Rice is Nice …Hmmmm!

A Selection
of
Easy to Cook
Rice Dishes

First published in 2015 by

Beecroft Publishing

Beecroft
Crittenden Road
Matfield
Kent
TN12 7EQ
United Kingdom

www.beecroftpublishing.co.uk
email: sales@beecroftpublishing.co.uk

ISBN 978-0-9546186-5-0

Copyright © 2015 Eddie Martin

All rights reserved around the world. This publication is copyright and may not be reproduced, in whole or in part, in any manner (except for excerpts thereof for bona fida purposes in accordance with the Copyright Act) without the prior permission in writing from Beecroft Publishing.

Disclaimer:
The information in this publication is distributed on as "as is" basis, without warranty. While every effort has been made to ensure that this book is free from errors and omissions, neither the author, the publisher, or their respective employees and agents, shall have any liability to any person or entity with respect to any liability, loss or damage caused or alleged to have been caused directly or indirectly by advice or instructions contained in this book.

Contents

Introduction 5
A Selection of Rice 7
The Variety of Pulses 9
Types of Onions 14
Types of Garlic 15
The Collection of Spices 16
Variety of Meats 17
Vegetable Selection 18
Other Ingredients 19
The Recipes 21
    Plain Boiled Rice 23
    Aduki Bean Rice 25
    Alubia Bean Rice 27
    American Haricot Bean Rice 29
    Australian Alubia Bean Rice 31
    Black Bean Rice 33
    Black Eye Bean Rice 35
    Borlotti Bean Rice 37
    Broad Bean Rice 39
    Butter Bean Rice 41
    Cannellini Bean Rice 43
    Chick Pea Rice 45
    Chinese Black Bean Rice 47
    Chinese Mung Bean Rice 49
    Flageolet Bean Rice 51
    French Puy Lentils and Rice 53
    Green Lentils and Rice 55
    Haricot Bean Rice 57
    Indian Green Lentils and Rice 59
    Indonesian Soya Bean Rice 61
    Italian Borlotti Bean Rice 63
    Italian Cannellini Bean Rice 65
    Japanese Aduki Bean Rice 67
    Kidney Bean Rice 69
    Latin Split Pea Rice 71
    Mediterranean Butter Bean Rice 73
    Mediterranean Flageolet Bean Rice 75
    Mexican Kidney Bean Rice 77
    Mung Bean Rice 79
    Pigeon Pea Rice 81
    Pinto Bean Rice 83
    Puy Lentils and Rice 85
    Red Lentils and Rice 87
    South American Broad Bean Rice 89
    Soya Bean Rice 91
    Spanish Pinto Bean Rice 93
    Split Pea Rice 95
    Sri Lankan Chick Pea Rice 97

Thai Red Lentils and Rice 99
West Indian Black Eye Bean Rice 101
West Indian Pigeon Pea Rice 103
Do It Yourself Recipes 104
Index 108

Introduction

Welcome to my book of exotic rice dishes. The name '**Rice is Nice ...Hmmmm!**' aptly describes what you should expect from cooking any of these rice dishes. You will find the look of the dish, the smell of the dish and most of all the taste of the dish will want to make you go 'Hmmmm! I want more'. However, before you go 'Hmmmm! I want more', we first have to cook the dishes.

This book was written to present you with different types of rice dishes that are truly exotic and from around the world. I grew up in Guyana, South America, and many of their colloquial dishes use rice and pulses. In fact, most countries in that part of the world, where rice is the staple diet, have similar colloquial dishes. These form the basis of many of my dishes, which I would like to share with you.

Before we begin to cook, there are a few basics you should know:

a) Cooking is flexible. Many people may not like some of the ingredients in the dishes. My view is 'Do not put anything in the dish that you do not like, why spoil it for you'. Quite a broad statement that, but remember, any ingredient you leave out of a dish will change the flavour that I had intended the dish to have. It is entirely up to you.

b) All the dishes are based on using different pulses, which add to the flavour of the dishes. The pulse is also used to name the dish. There is one exception, **Plain Boiled Rice**, which I have included as an extra recipe. You would be surprised how many people cannot cook plain boiled rice.

c) The word '**Meats**' is used as a generic term for **Beef**, **Chicken**, **Sausages**, **Gammon**, **Lamb**, **Pork** and **Prawns**.

d) **Vegetarians** – Every ingredient used except for the meats are non-animal extracts. Simply leave out the 'meat' when cooking. The dishes will still have the dominant taste of the pulses.

e) Meat Eaters – The recipe for the dishes include meat. You may wish to substitute any of the meats mentioned, if you desire. That's the beauty about cooking, a different meat will give a different flavour, why not try it.

f) **Rice** - I always use **Basmati Rice** or **Long Grain Rice** as they are most appropriate to my recipes. There is a chapter on the different types of rice and you may like to try some of the others mentioned.

g) **Onions** and **Garlic** – These two ingredients are always used in the dishes. In my opinion they are essential to any cooking and will add to the basic taste of the dish.

Enough of rules.

I have included a short chapter on each of the following. They describe the ingredients to make you aware of what you will be using in the dishes. The chapters on 'Rice' and 'Pulses' show you pictures of what the rice or pulse look like, a description of the item, cooking times and other information on the item.

Rice – the different varieties
Pulses – different types and how to cook them
Onions – types of onions
Garlic – types and forms of garlic
Spices – the various spices used
Meats – the various meats used
Vegetables – a variety used in the recipes
Other Ingredients – other ingredients used in the recipes

The remaining pages of the book are dedicated to the recipes and describe 'Cooking the Dishes'. Each recipe is on a separate page and is based on cooking for 4 people. On some of the facing pages are photographs of the cooked dishes, so you can see what they look like. The recipes refer to other parts of the book for relevant information, e.g. Rice, Pulses.

Enjoy cooking.

Eddie Martin

A Selection of Rice

There are many varieties of rice from around the world and they come in different shapes and colours. Rice is the most important crop in many countries providing the main economy as well as forming the basic stable diet. Rice can be made into different forms, e.g. cream of rice, pounded or flaked rice, noodles, flour, paper, milk and puffed rice. Not only is rice used in a variety of ways for varied cuisines but it is also involved in the culture of a country.

The origins of rice may never be known but it is widely believed that it originated in the Far East, possible between China and Thailand and is now grown all over the world. It is also believed that more people have used rice as a food source than any other crop in history.

Rice is normally classified by the size of the grain and as you will see from the table below, rice also has a variety of shapes and textures.

Photos	Types of Rice
	Arborio Rice – See **Risotto Rice**.
	Basmati Rice - An aromatic, **Long Grain Rice**. The grains swell almost three times lengthwise when cooked and are firm, dry, separate and fluffy. It has a unique flavour and aroma. Basmati Rice is available as **White Rice** or **Brown Rice**. Brown Basmati Rice has more fibre and a stronger flavour, and takes twice as long to cook.
	Botan Rice – See **Sweet Rice**.
	Brown Rice – Also known as **Whole Grain Rice**. The name and colour of the rice is due to the bran and germ layers, which surrounds the kernel. It is rich in minerals and vitamins and has a chewier and nuttier flavour than **White Rice**. It takes twice as long to cook than White Rice.
	Chinese Sweet Rice – See **Sweet Rice**.
	Glutinous Rice – See **Sweet Rice**.
	Indian Rice – See **Wild Rice**.
	Japanese Rice – See **Sweet Rice**.
	Jasmine Rice – Also known as **Thai Basmati Rice** or **Thai Jasmine Rice**. A **Long Grain Rice** that has an aromatic aroma and flavour of popcorn or nuts. It has a soft, moist texture that sticks together when cooked. The rice swells and one cup of dried rice will yield three cups of cooked rice. Jasmine Rice is available as **White Rice** or **Brown Rice**.
	Long Grain Rice - Long slender kernels that stay separate and fluffy when cooked. The length is four to five times longer than the width. There are several varieties of Long Grain Rice and it is the most common type of rice consumed in the world.

Photos	Types of Rice
	Medium Grain Rice – This rice has a shorter, wider kernel than **Long Grain Rice**. The cooked rice is stickier than Long Grain Rice by being more moist and tender, and is ideal for making paella and risottos. It is also known as **Calrose Rice**.
	Mochi Rice – See **Sweet Rice**.
	Paella Rice – Also known as **Spanish Rice**. A **Medium Grain Rice** that is very similar to **Risotto Rice**.
	Pearl Rice – See **Sweet Rice**.
	Pearled Rice – See **Short Grain Rice**.
	Piedmount Rice – See **Risotto Rice**.
	Risotto Rice – Also known as **Arborio Rice** and **Piedmount Rice**. A plump, **White Rice** that can absorb lots of water and not be soft. It will develop a firm center and a starchy outside when cooked.
	Round Grain Rice – See **Short Grain Rice**.
	Short Grain Rice – Also known as **Round Grain Rice** or **Pearled Rice**. It is short, plump and almost round. The cooked rice is soft and the grains stick together. It is ideal for rice puddings or sushi.
	Spanish Rice – See **Paella Rice**.
	Sticky Rice – See **Sweet Rice**.
	Sushi Rice – See **Sweet Rice**.
	Sweet Rice – Also known as **Glutinous Rice**, **Mochi Rice**, **Sushi Rice**, **Chinese Sweet Rice**, **Sticky Rice**, **Waxy Rice**, **Japanese Rice**, **Botan Rice** and **Pearl Rice**. The grain is short and plump with a chalky white, opaque colour. It is not sweet, does not contain gluten and loses its shape when cooked. One cup of the dried rice will yield two cups of the cooked rice. It is ideal for sushi, rice balls and desserts, and is available either as white or a rusty black colour.
	Thai Basmati Rice - See **Jasmine Rice**.
	Thai Jasmine Rice - See **Jasmine Rice**.
	Waxy Rice – See **Sweet Rice**.
	Whole Grain Rice – See **Brown Rice**.
	Wild Rice – Also known as **Indian Rice**. It is not classified as rice, but as a different type of grass. It is richer in protein and other nutrients than **White Rice** and has a nutty flavour. The rice comes with the bran on the grain, which makes it black in colour. It takes longer to cook than White Rice.

The Variety of Pulses

Use about 40gms of beans per person. However, you can use more or less as desired.

Dried pulses must be soaked in water before conventional cooking, i.e. not using a pressure cooker. Use about three times the amount of water as the pulse for soaking.

Long cold soak – All pulses, except for lentils, should be soaked in cold water for about 12 hours.

A quicker soaking method is to add three times the amount of water as the pulse, bring to the boil for a few minutes, remove from the heat and stand the pulse for an hour.

When cooking, either conventionally or by pressure cooker, add enough water to cover the beans by about 4cms or 1.5 inches. Always discard the water that the beans were cooked in. It is important for beans to be cooked until they are soft.

Use tinned beans if cooking the beans is not an option.

Photos	Pulse	Approx. size incr.	Conv. cooking time (mins.)	Pressure cooker (15psi) time (mins.)
	Aduki Beans – Also known as Adzuki or Azuki Beans. A small sweet flavoured red-brown bean from the adzuki plant. Used mainly in Asian cooking and in vegetarian dishes. The word 'Adzuki' originates from the Japanese 'azuki' meaning 'red bean'.	2-3	60	15
	Adzuki Beans see Aduki Beans.			
	Azuki Beans see Aduki Beans.			
	Alubia Beans – Also known as White Kidney Beans or Cannellini Beans. It has a nutty flavour and buttery texture.	2-3	60	15
	Black Beans – Also known as Turtle, Black Turtle, Mexican Black or Spanish Black Beans. A pea sized, black in colour bean with an earthy flavour used in Latin American, Chinese and Japanese dishes.	2-3	60	15

Photos	Pulse	Approx. size incr.	Conv. cooking time (mins.)	Pressure cooker (15psi) time (mins.)
	Black Eye Beans – Also known as Cowpeas. A small beige, kidney shaped bean with a black spot, which denotes its name. It has a scented aroma, creamy texture with a distinctive flavour.	3	50	15
	Black Turtle Beans see Black Beans.			
	Borlotti Beans – Also known as Cranberry, Roman, Resecoco, Shell, Christmas or Salugia Beans. A nutty flavoured speckled light brown bean normally used in Italian cuisine.	2	60	20
	Broad Beans – A green coloured bean with an earthy flavour.	2	10	n/a
	Butter Beans – Also known as Fava, Broad, Windsor or English Beans. A cream coloured bean with a soft texture and sweet earthy flavour.	2-3	45	7
	Cannellini Beans – Also known as Runner Cannellini, White Kidney or Fazolia beans. It has a smooth texture with a nutty flavour and used mainly in Italian cuisine.	2	60	15
	Chick Peas – Also called Garbanzo Beans. A round, pale yellow, nutty flavoured pea used in Asian and Middle eastern cuisines.	2	60	15
	Christmas Beans see Borlotti Beans.			
	Cranberry Beans see Borlotti Beans.			
	English Beans see Butter Beans.			

Photos	Pulse	Approx. size incr.	Conv. cooking time (mins.)	Pressure cooker (15psi) time (mins.)
	Fava Beans see Butter Beans.			
	Fayot Beans see Flageolet Beans.			
	Fazolia Beans see Cannellini Beans.			
	Flageolet Beans – Also known as Fayot Beans. A pale Green Bean with a creamy texture and delicate taste that comes in a slender pod.	2	90	20
	Garbanzo Beans see Chick Peas.			
	Green Gram Beans see Mung Beans.			
	Green Lentils – These are from the pea family, are lens shaped and come in different forms. There is the large seed type, pale green in colour, a smaller type whose colour is brown or almost black and the small type, which is reddish-orange in colour.	-	30	n/a
	Haricot Beans – A small white oval bean. They are used to make baked beans.	2	100	30
	Kidney Beans – Also known as Mexican or Rajma Beans. Normally red in colour with a meaty flavour. There is also a larger variety coloured black or white.	2	60	15
	Lima Beans – Also known as Madagascar Beans.	2-3	60	20
	Madagascar Beans see Lima Beans.			
	Mexican Beans see Kidney Beans.			

Photos	Pulse	Approx. size incr.	Conv. cooking time (mins.)	Pressure cooker (15psi) time (mins.)
	Mexican Black Beans see Black Beans.			
	Mung Beans – Also known as Mung Peas, Mungo beans or Green Gram Beans. These have a green skin, are slightly sweet and are used to grow bean sprouts, which are mainly used in Oriental cooking and salads.	2-3	45	15
	Mung Peas see Mung Beans.			
	Mungo Beans see Mung Beans.			
	Pigeon Peas – Also known as Gunga Peas or Congo Peas. A greenish-light brown pea very similar in size and shape to the Green Pea.	3	50	20
	Pinto Beans – A mottled brown and pink kidney shaped bean with a smooth texture.	2	60	20
	Puy Lentils – A small lentil, dark blue-green in colour with a distinctive taste.	-	30	n/a
	Rajma Beans see Kidney Beans.			
	Red Lentils – These are from the pea family, are lens shaped and come in different forms. There is the large seed type, pale green in colour, a smaller type whose colour is brown or almost black and the small type, which is reddish-orange in colour.	-	n/a Will cook with the rice	n/a
	Resecoco Beans see Borlotti Beans.			
	Roman Beans see Borlotti Beans.			

Photos	Pulse	Approx. size incr.	Conv. cooking time (mins.)	Pressure cooker (15psi) time (mins.)
	Runner Cannellini see Cannellini Beans.			
	Salugia Beans see Borlotti Beans.			
	Shell Beans see Borlotti Beans.			
	Soy Beans see Soya Beans.			
	Soya Beans – Also known as Soy Beans. A round beige coloured bean. Soya sauce, Miso soup and Tofu are a few items made from the Soya Bean.	2-3	120	30
	Spanish Black Beans see Black Beans.			
	Split Peas – A dried pea that is split in half. These are either green or yellow.	-	40	10
	Turtle Beans see Black Beans.			
	White Kidney Beans see Cannellini Beans.			
	Windsor Beans see Butter Beans.			

Types of Onions

Onions have two classifications. **Spring Onions**, which are fresh and used in salads and lightly cooked dishes, and **Conventional Onions** which can be stored for a longer period of time and are the ones used in most cooked dishes.

Conventional Onions are available in yellow, red or white. The yellow type onion makes up the greatest percentage of onions used in the world and will be used in the recipes. All onions have multiple outer layers of papery skin. Most have a strong pungent smell and flavour, and are ideal for savoury rice dishes.

Onions vary in size from 2cm to more than 9cm in diameter. The most common sizes of onions are medium (4 to 6 cm in diameter) and large (6 to 8 cm in diameter).

Yellow Onions have a strong-flavour, and turn brown when fried. **Red Onions** are ideal for fresh cooking and salads because of its colour. **White Onions** have a sweet flavour and turn a golden colour when fried.

There is not one known source where the onion originated. It is believed that wild onions have been grown for a very long time and that cultivation may have started about 5000 years ago.

Types of Garlic

There are many varieties of garlic in the world and they vary in colour from white to a dark wine colour. Garlic is a member of the lilies, **Onions**, leeks and **Chives** plant family and has been cultivated for thousands of years for its culinary and medicinal attributes.

The garlic plant can grow up to 50 cm and have flat green leaves. The plant has slender stalks, which produce edible flowers when in bloom. The skin of the garlic bulb encloses a number of cloves, which are used in cooking.

Garlic has been grown for about 5000 years and is one of the oldest known cultivated crops. There are other plants known as wild garlic. These are not necessary garlic itself but other species of the garlic family.

Garlic is available in different forms:-

Garlic bulbs and cloves – The fresh garlic normally bought.

Granulated Garlic - This provides the flavour but not the texture of fresh garlic and dissolves well in liquids.

Garlic flakes – These are dried pieces of garlic, which when mixed with a liquid provide the flavour and texture of fresh garlic.

Garlic powder – This provides the flavour of garlic but not the texture. It dissolves in liquids.

Garlic salt – A mixture of garlic powder and salt.

Garlic juice - Strained juice from minced or pressed garlic.

Garlic greens – The sprouts from a garlic bulb.

Garlic oil – Garlic cloves and **Olive Oil** heated together. The cloves are then taken out.

Elephant Garlic – This is milder than ordinary garlic. It is more a member of the leek plant family but looks like a very large garlic bulb.

The Collection of Spices

Ground and dried leaf spices are used for these rice dishes. All the ingredients are cooked in one pot and dried spices are more suitable when boiled with rice.

Spice	Description
Allspice	A flavour and aroma that resembles a combination of Nutmeg, Cinnamon and Cloves.
Basil	Basil has a fragrantly sweet bouquet with a slightly bitter and musty flavour.
Bay Leaf	An aromatic leaf with a woody flavour.
Black Pepper	Black Pepper adds flavour to almost all foods. It is pungent and aromatic, and is its taste is biting and hot.
Cayenne	Hot tasting pepper grounded from the pods and seeds of several kinds of dried Chilli Peppers.
Chilli Peppers	Chilli Peppers make any food hot and pungent.
Chinese Five Spice	A powder with a strong pungent aniseed flavour and aroma, consisting of grounded Cinnamon, Cloves, Fennel Seeds, Star Anise and Szechwan Pepper or Ginger.
Chives	Chives have a mild onion flavour with a hint of **Garlic**.
Cloves	Strong, pungent and sweet aroma and flavour.
Coriander	Also known as Cilantro. It has a mild, distinctive taste similar to a blend of Sage and Lemon.
Cumin	An Indian spice with an earthy flavour, which has a distinctive, slightly bitter yet warm flavour.
Curry Powder	A spice mixture, usually consisting of turmeric, Coriander, Fenugreek, Cumin, and Chilli Peppers.
Ginger	Ginger has a rich, sweet, warm and woody aroma with a slightly biting and hot taste.
Marjoram	Marjoram has an aromatic minty sweet flavour with a slight bitter taste.
Mustard Powder	Mustard Seeds are grounded to make the Mustard Powder. It has no aroma when dry, but produces a hot flavour when mixed with water.
Nutmeg	Nutmeg has an aromatic aroma with a slightly warm taste.
Oregano	Oregano has a strong aromatic and a slightly bitter pungent flavour.
Paprika	Paprika is a fine powder ground from the sweet variety of red **Capsicum Peppers**. It has a mild aroma with a bitter pungent flavour.
Parsley	This is the flat leaf type, also known as Italian Parsley, which has a pungent taste.
Rosemary	Rosemary has a sweet, fresh, pine aroma with a strong bittersweet flavour.
Salt	Salt brings out the flavour of meats, vegetables and any bland starchy foods.
Thyme	Thyme has a strong pungent fragrance and flavour, and ideal to mix with starchy foods.

Variety of Meats

As mentioned before, the word 'meats' is used as a generic term for Beef, Chicken, Sausages, Gammon, Lamb, Pork and Prawns.

Vegetarians – All the dishes in this book can be made without the meats. They do add to the flavour of the dish but you will still savour the dominant taste, which is from the pulses.

In the recipes various meats are used. However, meats are a personal and optional choice and may be changed to your own preference. Why not try a combination of meats, it's your choice.

Meat	Choosing	Preparation
Beef	**Rump Steak** or best braising/stewing steak	Cut into 1.5-2cms cubes
Chicken	Breasts are best	Cut into slices 1x4cms
Chorizo Sausage	Spanish – 2cms thick	Cut into slices 1cm thick
Gammon	Smoked is best	Cut into 1.5-2cms cubes
Lamb	**Loin of Lamb, Chump Chops** or **Chops** without the bone	Cut into 1.5-2cms cubes
Pork	**Loin of Pork**, chops without the bone	Cut into 1.5-2cms cubes
Prawns	Large ones are best	Shelled

Please ensure that all meats are properly cooked, especially **chicken**. While cooking, cut the meat to see if it is still uncooked on the inside. If in doubt, cook the meat until it is golden brown.

Vegetable Selection

All vegetables used should be fresh and firm except for some mentioned in the table below.

Vegetables	Choosing	Preparation
Capsicum Peppers	Although not strictly a vegetable - Red, yellow and green	Cut into slices 1-2cms long
Carrots	Fresh	Peel the skin and dice into half centimetre cubes
Garlic	Firm to the touch. See 'Garlic' chapter.	Peel and chop
Green Beans	Fresh	Discard the ends and cut into pieces 1-2cms long
Green Peas	Fresh	Take out from the pod.
	Frozen	Defrost
Mushrooms	Any fresh type	Cut into slices
Onions	Fresh and firm **Yellow Onions**. See 'Onions' chapter.	Peel and chop
Sweet Corn	Tinned	Strain liquid
Tomatoes	Chopped tinned	Use as is
	Fresh	Chopped

Other Ingredients

Ingredients	Choosing	Preparation
Brown Sugar	**Demerara Sugar**	Use as is
Coconut Milk	Tinned	Use as is
	Mature coconut	Crack open the coconut and prise out the hard coconut flesh. The water that comes from the coconut is NOT the milk, as many people believe. Grate the coconut flesh into fine pieces and soak in 2 cups of hot water for about an hour. Pummel and squeeze the coconut mixture with your hands until the water turns very milky. The result is the coconut milk. Strain the milk off into a container.
Corn Oil	Bottled	Use as is
Fish Sauce	Bottled	Use as is
Lemon Juice	Fresh	Squeeze lemon to extract juice without the pips.
	Bottled	Use as is
Lemon Zest	Fresh	Grate the skin of a lemon
Lime Juice	Fresh	Squeeze lime to extract the juice without the pips.
	Bottle	Use as is
Olive Oil	Bottled – virgin	Use as is
Orange Zest	Fresh	Grate the skin of the orange
Sesame Oil	Bottled	Use as is
Soy Sauce	Bottled	Use as is
Stock Cube	Packet	Crumble a stock cube.
	Fresh	Make your own
Tomato Puree	Any	Use as is
Vegetable Oil	Bottled	Use as is

Blank Page

The Recipes

Plain Boiled Rice

Plain Boiled Rice

(Time to cook = 12 minutes)

This is one of the easiest dishes to prepare. There are no secrets to making plain boiled rice and many people seem to have problems cooking it. Yes, there are different methods of cooking rice and this method will show how to make perfect plain boiled rice every time.

The method described below is ideal for **Basmati Rice** or **Long Grain Rice**.

First of all, decide on how much rice to prepare. How many people is the rice being prepared for, or is it being added to another dish. The quantities may vary depending on the reason and also the type of rice. Some rice swell up more than others when cooked. As a rule, use 80gms or half a cup of the uncooked rice for each person.

Most rice is pre-washed these days, but to get rid of the extra starch wash it again in cold water. This is not compulsory.

Select a pot that will be sufficient in size to hold the swelled rice. Fill the pot to just over half way with water. Add salt to taste and bring to the boil. Put the rice into the pot and stir with a fork to avoid it sticking initially. Turn the heat down to simmer and stir occasionally.

Now this is where people have difficulty. How to know when the rice is cooked? Is there enough water in the pot? Don't worry about the water. This method ensures there is always enough water in the pot. A kettle of boiled water should be available to add water to the pot and to keep the rice submerged.

After about 10 minutes, use the fork to extract a couple of grains of rice from the pot. Squeeze the rice to see if it is soft, try it in your mouth if necessary. The rice should not be grainy (hard on the inside) and neither should it be too soft and mushy. A medium point is when the rice is firm but not grainy on the inside. Repeat this test often.

Once cooked, strain the rice but do not wash under running water. That washes away goodness. Let the rice 'drip dry'.

There are choices now on how to keep and serve the rice hot:

a) After straining the rice in the sieve, put some water back into the pot (about 2 cm). Rest the sieve on the pot and put back onto the cooker to simmer. Cover the rice with the pot lid and the rice will steam when the water boils. Ensure the pot does not boil dry of water.
b) Put the 'drip dried' rice in a suitable covered container and place in the oven at 180c. This will keep the rice hot and fluffy.
c) Put the 'drip dried' rice in a suitable covered container and place in the microwave oven. Set for the required amount of time for the quantity of rice. This will make the rice hot and fluffy.

There it is - fluffy, separated, plain boiled rice.

Aduki Bean Rice

Aduki Bean Rice

Serves 4 - (Time to prepare and cook = 1 hour)

160gms **Aduki Beans** – soaked and cooked
80gms or half a cup of **Basmati Rice** per person
1 large **Onion** – chopped
4 cloves of **Garlic** – chopped
1 litre of hot water
150gms **Green Beans** – cut into small pieces
150gms tinned **Sweet Corn**
400ml can **Coconut Milk**, or grate, soak and squeeze the milk from one coconut
150gms red **Capsicum Pepper** – cut into small pieces
600gms **Chicken** – cut into cubes
3 teaspoons **Marjoram**
3 teaspoons **Chives**   2 teaspoons of **Salt**
6 tablespoons **Corn Oil**   1 teaspoon of **Black Pepper**

Soak the Aduki Beans overnight in three times the amount of water to the volume of beans when cooking them by conventional cooking, i.e. not using a pressure cooker.

Select a large pot for cooking that will be sufficient for all the ingredients, including the swollen rice when cooked. A 4-5 litre pot will be ample.

Cook the Aduki Beans as indicated in the 'Pulses' chapter. The cooking time depends on whether a pot and lid (conventional) or a pressure cooker is used. The beans are cooked when they can be squashed between two fingers without them being too hard or too soft. Discard the water and transfer the beans into a suitable container for later use.

Heat the oil and fry the onion for about 3 minutes, stirring occasionally. Add the garlic and fry for another minute, stirring occasionally.

Add the Marjoram, Chives, salt, black pepper and fry for another minute to let the flavour of the spices infuse into the oil. Stir occasionally.

Add the chicken and continue to fry until the chicken is cooked. Stir occasionally to ensure the chicken is cooked all over.

Add the water, rice, cooked beans, green beans and coconut milk. Bring to the boil, reduce the heat and simmer for about 8 minutes, stirring occasionally.

Add the sweet corn, red pepper and simmer on a very low heat until the rice is cooked, stirring occasionally. The rice will soak up the water and coconut milk. If the water has evaporated before the rice is cooked, add small amounts of water to ensure the rice is cooked. Occasionally pinch the rice between two fingers to test if it is ready. It needs to be firm but soft, i.e. not gritty on the inside.

Alubia Bean Rice

Alubia Bean Rice

Serves 4 - (Time to prepare and cook = 1 hour)

160gms **Alubia Beans** – soaked and cooked
80gms or half a cup of **Basmati Rice** per person
1 large **Onion** – chopped
4 cloves of **Garlic** – chopped
1.5 litres of hot water
400gms chopped tinned **Tomatoes**
150gms **Green Beans** – cut into small pieces
150gms **Mushrooms** - chopped
150gms red **Capsicum Pepper** – cut into small pieces
600gms **Chorizo Sausage** – cut into cubes
3 teaspoons **Basil**
3 teaspoons **Thyme**   2 teaspoons of **Salt**
6 tablespoons **Corn Oil**   1 teaspoon of **Black Pepper**

Soak the Alubia Beans overnight in three times the amount of water to the volume of beans when cooking them by conventional cooking, i.e. not using a pressure cooker.

Select a large pot for cooking that will be sufficient for all the ingredients, including the swollen rice when cooked. A 4-5 litre pot will be ample.

Cook the Alubia Beans as indicated in the 'Pulses' chapter. The cooking time depends on whether a pot and lid (conventional) or a pressure cooker is used. The beans are cooked when they can be squashed between two fingers without them being too hard or too soft. Discard the water and transfer the beans into a suitable container for later use.

Heat the oil and fry the onion for about 3 minutes, stirring occasionally. Add the garlic and fry for another minute, stirring occasionally.

Add the Basil, Thyme, salt, black pepper and fry for another minute to let the flavour of the spices infuse into the oil. Stir occasionally.

Add the water, rice, cooked beans, Chorizo sausage, tomatoes, mushrooms and green beans. Bring to the boil, reduce the heat and simmer for about 8 minutes, stir occasionally.

Add the red pepper and simmer on a very low heat until the rice is cooked, stirring occasionally. The rice will soak up the water. If the water has evaporated before the rice is cooked, add small amounts of water to ensure the rice is cooked. Occasionally pinch the rice between two fingers to test if it is ready. It needs to be firm but soft, i.e. not gritty on the inside.

Haricot Beans

American Haricot Bean Rice

Serves 4 - (Time to prepare and cook = 1 hour)

160gms **Haricot Beans** – soaked and cooked
80gms or half a cup of **Basmati Rice** per person
1 large **Onion** – chopped
4 cloves of **Garlic** – chopped
1.5 litres of hot water
400gms chopped tinned **Tomatoes**
150gms **Green Beans** – cut into small pieces
150gms tinned **Sweet Corn**

600gms **Lamb** – cut into cubes	1 teaspoon ground **Cumin**
1 teaspoon **Paprika**	1 teaspoon **Thyme**
1 teaspoon **Cayenne**	2 teaspoons **Brown Sugar**
1 teaspoon **Oregano**	2 teaspoons of **Salt**
6 tablespoons **Corn Oil**	1 teaspoon of **Black Pepper**

Soak the Haricot Beans overnight in three times the amount of water to the volume of beans when cooking them by conventional cooking, i.e. not using a pressure cooker.

Select a large pot for cooking that will be sufficient for all the ingredients, including the swollen rice when cooked. A 4-5 litre pot will be ample.

Cook the Haricot Beans as indicated in the 'Pulses' chapter. The cooking time depends on whether a pot and lid (conventional) or a pressure cooker is used. The beans are cooked when they can be squashed between two fingers without them being too hard or too soft. Discard the water and transfer the beans into a suitable container for later use.

Heat the oil and fry the onion for about 3 minutes, stirring occasionally. Add the garlic and fry for another minute, stirring occasionally.

Add the Paprika, ground Cumin, Cayenne, Thyme, Oregano, sugar, salt, black pepper and fry for another minute to let the flavour of the spices infuse into the oil. Stir occasionally.

Add the lamb and continue to fry until the lamb is cooked. Stir occasionally to ensure the lamb is cooked all over.

Add the water, rice, cooked beans, tomatoes and green beans. Bring to the boil, reduce the heat on the cooker and simmer for about 8 minutes. Stir occasionally.

Add the sweet corn and simmer on a very low heat until the rice is cooked, stirring occasionally. The rice will soak up the water. If the water has evaporated before the rice is cooked, add small amounts of water to ensure the rice is cooked. Occasionally pinch the rice between two fingers to test if it is ready. It needs to be firm but soft, i.e. not gritty on the inside.

Alubia Beans

Australian Alubia Bean Rice

Serves 4 - (Time to prepare and cook = 1 hour)

160gms **Alubia Beans** – soaked and cooked
80gms or half a cup of **Basmati Rice** per person
1 large **Onion** – chopped
4 cloves of **Garlic** – chopped
1.5 litres of hot water
400gms chopped tinned **Tomatoes**
150gms **Green Peas**
150gms diced **Carrots**
600gms **Pork** – cut into cubes
3 teaspoons **Basil**
3 teaspoons **Oregano**   2 teaspoons of **Salt**
6 tablespoons **Corn Oil**   1 teaspoon of **Black Pepper**
3 teaspoons **Brown Sugar**   Zest of 1 **Lemon**

Soak the Alubia Beans overnight in three times the amount of water to the volume of beans when cooking them by conventional cooking, i.e. not using a pressure cooker.

Select a large pot for cooking that will be sufficient for all the ingredients, including the swollen rice when cooked. A 4-5 litre pot will be ample.

Cook the Alubia Beans as indicated in the 'Pulses' chapter. The cooking time depends on whether a pot and lid (conventional) or a pressure cooker is used. The beans are cooked when they can be squashed between two fingers without them being too hard or too soft. Discard the water and transfer the beans into a suitable container for later use.

Heat the oil and fry the onion for about 3 minutes, stirring occasionally. Add the garlic and fry for another minute, stirring occasionally.

Add the Basil, Oregano, salt, black pepper, brown sugar, zest of lemon and fry for another minute to let the flavour of the spices infuse into the oil. Stir occasionally.

Add the pork and continue to fry until the pork is cooked. Stir occasionally to ensure the pork is cooked all over.

Add the water, rice, cooked beans, tomatoes, green peas, carrots and simmer on a very low heat until the rice is cooked, stirring occasionally. The rice will soak up the water. If the water has evaporated before the rice is cooked, add small amounts of water to ensure the rice is cooked. Occasionally pinch the rice between two fingers to test if it is ready. It needs to be firm but soft, i.e. not gritty on the inside.

Black Bean Rice

Black Bean Rice

Serves 4 - (Time to prepare and cook = 1 hour)

160gms **Black Beans** – soaked and cooked
80gms or half a cup of **Basmati Rice** per person
1 large **Onion** – chopped
4 cloves of **Garlic** – chopped
1.5 litres of hot water
150gms tinned **Sweet Corn**
150gms diced **Carrots**
150gms green **Capsicum Pepper** – cut into small pieces
600gms **Pork** – cut into cubes
3 teaspoons **Oregano**
3 teaspoons **Thyme**   2 teaspoons of **Salt**
6 tablespoons **Corn Oil**   1 teaspoon of **Black Pepper**

Soak the Black Beans overnight in three times the amount of water to the volume of beans when cooking them by conventional cooking, i.e. not using a pressure cooker.

Select a large pot for cooking that will be sufficient for all the ingredients, including the swollen rice when cooked. A 4-5 litre pot will be ample.

Cook the Black Beans as indicated in the 'Pulses' chapter. The cooking time depends on whether a pot and lid (conventional) or a pressure cooker is used. The beans are cooked when they can be squashed between two fingers without them being too hard or too soft. Discard the water and transfer the beans into a suitable container for later use.

Heat the oil and fry the onion for about 3 minutes, stirring occasionally. Add the garlic and fry for another minute, stirring occasionally.

Add the Oregano, Thyme, salt, black pepper and fry for another minute to let the flavour of the spices infuse into the oil. Stir occasionally.

Add the pork and continue to fry until the pork is cooked. Stir occasionally to ensure the pork is cooked all over.

Add the water, rice, cooked beans, carrots and bring to the boil. Reduce the heat on the cooker and simmer for about 8 minutes, stirring occasionally.

Add the sweet corn, green pepper and simmer on a very low heat until the rice is cooked, stirring occasionally. The rice will soak up the water. If the water has evaporated before the rice is cooked, add small amounts of water to ensure the rice is cooked. Occasionally pinch the rice between two fingers to test if it is ready. It needs to be firm but soft, i.e. not gritty on the inside.

Black Eye Bean Rice

Black Eye Bean Rice

Serves 4 - (Time to prepare and cook = 1.5 hours)

160gms **Black Eye Beans** – soaked and cooked
80gms or half a cup of **Basmati Rice** per person
1 large **Onion** – chopped
4 cloves of **Garlic** – chopped
1 litre of hot water
400gms chopped tinned **Tomatoes**
400ml can **Coconut Milk**, or grate, soak and squeeze the milk from one coconut
150gms red **Capsicum Pepper** – cut into small pieces
4 small **Chilli Peppers** – chopped or grounded
300gms smoked **Gammon**   300gms cooked **Prawns**
3 teaspoons **Marjoram**   3 teaspoons **Thyme**
6 tablespoons **Corn Oil**   2 teaspoons of **Salt**
1 teaspoon of **Black Pepper**

Soak the Black Eye Beans overnight in three times the amount of water to the volume of beans when cooking them by conventional cooking, i.e. not using a pressure cooker.

Select a large pot for cooking that will be sufficient for all the ingredients, including the swollen rice when cooked. A 4-5 litre pot will be ample.

Boil the gammon in water for about half an hour until cooked. Cool and cut the gammon into small cubes.

Cook the Black Eye Beans as indicated in the 'Pulses' chapter. The cooking time depends on whether a pot and lid (conventional) or a pressure cooker is used. The beans are cooked when they can be squashed between two fingers without them being too hard or too soft. Discard the water and transfer the beans into a suitable container for later use.

Heat the oil and fry the onion for about 3 minutes, stirring occasionally. Add the garlic and fry for another minute, stirring occasionally.

Add the Marjoram, Thyme, chilli peppers, salt, black pepper and fry for another minute to let the flavour of the spices infuse into the oil. Stir occasionally.

Add the water, rice, cooked beans, tomatoes and coconut milk. Bring to the boil, reduce the heat and simmer for about 8 minutes, stirring occasionally.

Add the gammon, prawns and red pepper, and continue to simmer on a very low heat until the rice is cooked. Stir occasionally. The rice will soak up the water and coconut milk. If the water has evaporated before the rice is cooked, add small amounts of water to ensure the rice is cooked. Occasionally pinch the rice between two fingers to test if it is ready. It needs to be firm but soft, i.e. not gritty on the inside.

Borlotti Bean Rice

Borlotti Bean Rice

Serves 4 - (Time to prepare and cook = 1 hour)

160gms **Borlotti Beans** – soaked and cooked
80gms or half a cup of **Basmati Rice** per person
1 large **Onion** – chopped
4 cloves of **Garlic** – chopped
1.5 litres of hot water
400gms chopped tinned **Tomatoes**
150gms **Green Peas**
150gms yellow **Capsicum Pepper** – cut into small pieces
600gms **Beef** – cut into cubes (see variety of meats chapter)
3 teaspoons **Marjoram**
3 teaspoons **Oregano**   2 teaspoons of **Salt**
6 tablespoons **Corn Oil**   1 teaspoon of **Black Pepper**

Soak the Borlotti Beans overnight in three times the amount of water to the volume of beans when cooking them by conventional cooking, i.e. not using a pressure cooker.

Select a large pot for cooking that will be sufficient for all the ingredients, including the swollen rice when cooked. A 4-5 litre pot will be ample.

Cook the Borlotti Beans as indicated in the 'Pulses' chapter. The cooking time depends on whether a pot and lid (conventional) or a pressure cooker is used. The beans are cooked when they can be squashed between two fingers without them being too hard or too soft. Discard the water and transfer the beans into a suitable container for later use.

Heat the oil and fry the onion for about 3 minutes, stirring occasionally. Add the garlic and fry for another minute, stirring occasionally.

Add the Marjoram, Oregano, salt, black pepper and fry for another minute to let the flavour of the spices infuse into the oil. Stir occasionally.

Add the beef and continue to fry until the beef is cooked. Stir occasionally to ensure the beef is cooked all over.

Add the water, rice, cooked beans, tomatoes, green peas and bring to the boil. Reduce the heat on the cooker and simmer for about 8 minutes, stirring occasionally.

Add the yellow pepper and simmer on a very low heat until the rice is cooked, stirring occasionally. The rice will soak up the water. If the water has evaporated before the rice is cooked, add small amounts of water to ensure the rice is cooked. Occasionally pinch the rice between two fingers to test if it is ready. It needs to be firm but soft, i.e. not gritty on the inside.

Broad Bean Rice

Broad Bean Rice

Serves 4 - (Time to prepare and cook = 1 hour)

160gms **Broad Beans** – fresh and cooked
80gms or half a cup of **Basmati Rice** per person
1 large **Onion** – chopped
4 cloves of **Garlic** – chopped
1.5 litres of hot water
400gms chopped tinned **Tomatoes**
150gms **Green Beans** – cut into small pieces
150gms **Mushrooms** - chopped
150gms yellow **Capsicum Pepper** – cut into small pieces
600gms **Beef** – cut into cubes (see variety of meats chapter)
3 teaspoons **Oregano**
3 teaspoons **Chives**   2 teaspoons of **Salt**
6 tablespoons **Corn Oil**   1 teaspoon of **Black Pepper**

Select a large pot for cooking that will be sufficient for all the ingredients, including the swollen rice when cooked. A 4-5 litre pot will be ample.

Cook the fresh Broad Beans as indicated in the 'Pulses' chapter. As the beans are fresh, they should be cooked by conventional means, i.e. pot and lid. The beans are cooked when they can be squashed between two fingers without them being too hard or too soft. Discard the water and transfer the beans into a suitable container for later use.

Heat the oil and fry the onion for about 3 minutes, stirring occasionally. Add the garlic and fry for another minute, stirring occasionally.

Add the Oregano, Chives, salt, black pepper and fry for another minute to let the flavour of the spices infuse into the oil. Stir occasionally.

Add the beef and continue to fry until the beef is cooked. Stir occasionally to ensure the beef is cooked all over.

Add the water, rice, cooked beans, tomatoes, green beans, mushrooms and bring to the boil. Reduce the heat on the cooker and simmer for about 8 minutes, stirring occasionally.

Add the yellow pepper and simmer on a very low heat until the rice is cooked, stirring occasionally. The rice will soak up the water. If the water has evaporated before the rice is cooked, add small amounts of water to ensure the rice is cooked. Occasionally pinch the rice between two fingers to test if it is ready. It needs to be firm but soft, i.e. not gritty on the inside.

Butter Bean Rice

Butter Bean Rice

Serves 4 - (Time to prepare and cook = 1 hour)

160gms **Butter Beans** – soaked and cooked
80gms or half a cup of **Basmati Rice** per person
1 large **Onion** – chopped
4 cloves of **Garlic** – chopped
1.5 litres of hot water
400gms chopped tinned **Tomatoes**
150gms **Mushrooms** - chopped
150gms **Green Peas**
150gms red **Capsicum Pepper** – cut into small pieces
600gms **Chorizo Sausage** – cut into cubes
3 teaspoons **Oregano**
3 teaspoons **Thyme**
6 tablespoons **Corn Oil**
2 teaspoons of **Salt**
1 teaspoon of **Black Pepper**

Soak the Butter Beans overnight in three times the amount of water to the volume of beans when cooking them by conventional cooking, i.e. not using a pressure cooker.

Select a large pot for cooking that will be sufficient for all the ingredients, including the swollen rice when cooked. A 4-5 litre pot will be ample.

Cook the Butter Beans as indicated in the 'Pulses' chapter. The cooking time depends on whether a pot and lid (conventional) or a pressure cooker is used. The beans are cooked when they can be squashed between two fingers without them being too hard or too soft. Discard the water and transfer the beans into a suitable container for later use.

Heat the oil and fry the onion for about 3 minutes, stirring occasionally. Add the garlic and fry for another minute, stirring occasionally.

Add the Oregano, Thyme, salt, black pepper and fry for another minute to let the flavour of the spices infuse into the oil. Stir occasionally.

Add the water, rice, cooked beans, Chorizo sausage, tomatoes, mushrooms, green peas and bring to the boil. Reduce the heat on the cooker and simmer for about 8 minutes, stirring occasionally.

Add the red pepper and simmer on a very low heat until the rice is cooked, stirring occasionally. The rice will soak up the water and coconut milk. If the water has evaporated before the rice is cooked, add small amounts of water to ensure the rice is cooked. Occasionally pinch the rice between two fingers to test if it is ready. It needs to be firm but soft, i.e. not gritty on the inside.

Cannellini Bean Rice

Cannellini Bean Rice

Serves 4 - (Time to prepare and cook = 1.5 hours)

160gms **Cannellini Beans** – soaked and cooked
80gms or half a cup of **Basmati Rice** per person
1 large **Onion** – chopped
4 cloves of **Garlic** – chopped
1.5 litres of hot water
400gms chopped tinned **Tomatoes**
150gms **Green Beans** – cut into small pieces
150gms **Mushrooms** - chopped
150gms red **Capsicum Pepper** – cut into small pieces
600gms smoked **Gammon**
3 teaspoons **Oregano**

3 teaspoons **Chives**	6 tablespoons **Corn Oil**
2 teaspoons of **Salt**	1 teaspoon of **Black Pepper**

Soak the Cannellini Beans overnight in three times the amount of water to the volume of beans when cooking them by conventional cooking, i.e. not using a pressure cooker.

Select a large pot for cooking that will be sufficient for all the ingredients, including the swollen rice when cooked. A 4-5 litre pot will be ample.

Boil the gammon in water for about half an hour until cooked. Cool and cut the gammon into small cubes.

Cook the Cannellini Beans as indicated in the 'Pulses' chapter. The cooking time depends on whether a pot and lid (conventional) or a pressure cooker is used. The beans are cooked when they can be squashed between two fingers without them being too hard or too soft. Discard the water and transfer the beans into a suitable container for later use.

Heat the oil and fry the onion for about 3 minutes, stirring occasionally. Add the garlic and fry for another minute, stirring occasionally.

Add the Oregano, Chives, salt, black pepper and fry for another minute to let the flavour of the spices infuse into the oil. Stir occasionally.

Add the water, rice, cooked beans, gammon, tomatoes, green beans, mushrooms and bring to the boil. Reduce the heat on the cooker and simmer for about 8 minutes, stirring occasionally.

Add the red pepper and continue to simmer on a very low heat until the rice is cooked. Stir occasionally. The rice will soak up the water. If the water has evaporated before the rice is cooked, add small amounts of water to ensure the rice is cooked. Occasionally pinch the rice between two fingers to test if it is ready. It needs to be firm but soft, i.e. not gritty on the inside.

Chick Pea Rice

Chick Pea Rice

Serves 4 - (Time to prepare and cook = 1.5 hours)

160gms **Chick Peas** – soaked and cooked
1 large **Onion** – chopped
400gms chopped tinned **Tomatoes**
150gms **Green Peas**
300gms smoked **Gammon**
3 teaspoons **Thyme**
2 teaspoons of **Salt**
1 litre of hot water
80gms or half a cup of **Basmati Rice** per person
4 cloves of **Garlic** – chopped
150gms **Mushrooms** – chopped
300gms **Chicken** – cut into cubes
3 teaspoons **Marjoram**
6 tablespoons **Corn Oil**
1 teaspoon of **Black Pepper**
400ml can **Coconut Milk**, or grate, soak and squeeze the milk from one coconut
150gms red **Capsicum Pepper** – cut into small pieces
4 small **Chilli Peppers** – chopped or grounded

Soak the Chick Peas overnight in three times the amount of water to the volume of peas.

Select a large pot for cooking that will be sufficient for all the ingredients, including the swollen rice when cooked. A 4-5 litre pot will be ample.

Boil the gammon in water for about half an hour until cooked. Cool and cut the gammon into small cubes.

Cook the Chick Peas as indicated in the 'Pulses' chapter. The cooking time depends on whether a pot and lid (conventional) or a pressure cooker is used. The peas are cooked when they can be squashed between two fingers without them being too hard or too soft. Discard the water and transfer the peas into a suitable container for later use.

Heat the oil and fry the onion for about 3 minutes, stirring occasionally. Add the garlic and fry for another minute, stirring occasionally.

Add the Marjoram, Thyme, chilli peppers, salt, black pepper and fry for another minute to let the flavour of the spices infuse into the oil. Stir occasionally.

Add the chicken and continue to fry until the chicken is cooked. Stir occasionally to ensure the chicken is cooked all over.

Add the water, cooked peas, green peas and coconut milk. Bring to the boil and reduce the heat on the cooker to simmer.

Add the rice, tomatoes, mushrooms, gammon and simmer for about 8 minutes. Stir occasionally.

Add the red pepper and continue to simmer on a very low heat until the rice is cooked. Stir occasionally. The rice will soak up the water and coconut milk. If the water has evaporated before the rice is cooked, add small amounts of water to ensure the rice is cooked. Occasionally pinch the rice between two fingers to test if it is ready. It needs to be firm but soft, i.e. not gritty on the inside.

Black Beans

Chinese Black Bean Rice

Serves 4 - (Time to prepare and cook = 1 hour)

160gms **Black Beans** – soaked and cooked
80gms or half a cup of **Basmati Rice** per person
1 large **Onion** – chopped
4 cloves of **Garlic** – chopped
1.5 litres of hot water
150gms **Green Beans** – cut into small pieces
150gms tinned **Sweet Corn**
600gms **Chicken** – cut into slices
4 teaspoons **Chinese Five Spice**
4 teaspoons **Soy Sauce**
6 tablespoons **Sesame Oil**
2 teaspoons of **Salt**
1 teaspoon of **Black Pepper**

Soak the Black Beans overnight in three times the amount of water to the volume of beans when cooking them by conventional cooking, i.e. not using a pressure cooker.

Select a large pot for cooking that will be sufficient for all the ingredients, including the swollen rice when cooked. A 4-5 litre pot will be ample.

Cook the Black Beans as indicated in the 'Pulses' chapter. The cooking time depends on whether a pot and lid (conventional) or a pressure cooker is used. The beans are cooked when they can be squashed between two fingers without them being too hard or too soft. Discard the water and transfer the beans into a suitable container for later use.

Heat the oil and fry the onion for about 3 minutes, stirring occasionally. Add the garlic and fry for another minute, stirring occasionally.

Add the Chinese Five Spice, salt, black pepper and fry for another minute to let the flavour of the spices infuse into the oil. Stir occasionally.

Add the chicken and continue to fry until the chicken is cooked. Stir occasionally to ensure the chicken is cooked all over.

Add the water and cooked beans. Bring to the boil and reduce the heat on the cooker to simmer.

Add the rice, green beans, sweet corn, soy sauce and simmer on a very low heat until the rice is cooked, stirring occasionally. The rice will soak up the water. If the water has evaporated before the rice is cooked, add small amounts of water to ensure the rice is cooked. Occasionally pinch the rice between two fingers to test if it is ready. It needs to be firm but soft, i.e. not gritty on the inside.

Mung Beans

Chinese Mung Bean Rice

Serves 4 - (Time to prepare and cook = 1 hour)

160gms **Mung Beans** – soaked and cooked
80gms or half a cup of **Basmati Rice** per person
1 large **Onion** – chopped
4 cloves of **Garlic** – chopped
1.5 litres of hot water
150gms **Mushrooms** - chopped
150gms yellow **Capsicum Pepper** – cut into small pieces
600gms cooked **Prawns**
4 teaspoons **Chinese Five Spice**
4 teaspoons **Soy Sauce**
3 tablespoons **Sesame Oil**
2 teaspoons of **Salt**
1 teaspoon of **Black Pepper**

Soak the Mung Beans overnight in three times the amount of water to the volume of beans when cooking them by conventional cooking, i.e. not using a pressure cooker.

Select a large pot for cooking that will be sufficient for all the ingredients, including the swollen rice when cooked. A 4-5 litre pot will be ample.

Cook the Mung Beans as indicated in the 'Pulses' chapter. The cooking time depends on whether a pot and lid (conventional) or a pressure cooker is used. The beans are cooked when they can be squashed between two fingers without them being too hard or too soft. Discard the water and transfer the beans into a suitable container for later use.

Heat the oil and fry the onion for about 3 minutes, stirring occasionally. Add the garlic and fry for another minute, stirring occasionally.

Add the Chinese Five Spice, salt, black pepper and fry for another minute to let the flavour of the spices infuse into the oil. Stir occasionally.

Add the water, rice, cooked beans and mushrooms. Bring to the boil, reduce the heat on the cooker and simmer for about 8 minutes. Stir occasionally.

Add the cooked prawns, yellow pepper and soy sauce. Continue to simmer on a very low heat until the rice is cooked. Stir occasionally. The rice will soak up the water. If the water has evaporated before the rice is cooked, add small amounts of water to ensure the rice is cooked. Occasionally pinch the rice between two fingers to test if it is ready. It needs to be firm but soft, i.e. not gritty on the inside.

Flageolet Bean Rice

Flageolet Bean Rice

Serves 4 - (Time to prepare and cook = 1 hour)

160gms **Flageolet Beans** – soaked and cooked
80gms or half a cup of **Basmati Rice** per person
400gms chopped tinned **Tomatoes**
150gms **Green Beans** – cut into small pieces
1 large **Onion** – chopped   4 cloves of **Garlic** – chopped
150gms **Mushrooms** – chopped   300gms **Chicken** – cut into cubes
300gms cooked **Prawns**   3 teaspoons **Marjoram**
3 teaspoons **Basil**   6 tablespoons **Corn Oil**
2 teaspoons of **Salt**   1 teaspoon of **Black Pepper**
1 litre of hot water
400ml can **Coconut Milk**, or grate, soak and squeeze the milk from one coconut
150gms red **Capsicum Pepper** – cut into small pieces

Soak the Flageolet Beans overnight in three times the amount of water to the volume of beans when cooking them by conventional cooking, i.e. not using a pressure cooker.

Select a large pot for cooking that will be sufficient for all the ingredients, including the swollen rice when cooked. A 4-5 litre pot will be ample.

Cook the Flageolet Beans as indicated in the 'Pulses' chapter. The cooking time depends on whether a pot and lid (conventional) or a pressure cooker is used. The beans are cooked when they can be squashed between two fingers without them being too hard or too soft. Discard the water and transfer the beans into a suitable container for later use.

Heat the oil and fry the onion for about 3 minutes, stirring occasionally. Add the garlic and fry for another minute, stirring occasionally.

Add the Marjoram, Basil, salt, black pepper and fry for another minute to let the flavour of the spices infuse into the oil. Stir occasionally.

Add the chicken and continue to fry until the chicken is cooked. Stir occasionally to ensure the chicken is cooked all over.

Add the water, rice, cooked beans, tomatoes, green beans, mushrooms and coconut milk. Bring to the boil, reduce the heat on the cooker and simmer for about 8 minutes. Stir occasionally.

Add the cooked prawns, red pepper and continue to simmer on a very low heat until the rice is cooked. Stir occasionally. The rice will soak up the water and coconut milk. If the water has evaporated before the rice is cooked, add small amounts of water to ensure the rice is cooked. Occasionally pinch the rice between two fingers to test if it is ready. It needs to be firm but soft, i.e. not gritty on the inside.

Puy Lentils

French Puy Lentils and Rice

Serves 4 - (Time to prepare and cook = 1 hour)

160gms **Puy Lentils**
80gms or half a cup of **Basmati Rice** per person
1 large **Onion** – chopped
4 cloves of **Garlic** – chopped
1.5 litres of hot water
400gms chopped tinned **Tomatoes**
150gms **Green Beans** – cut into small pieces
150gms red **Capsicum Pepper** – cut into small pieces
600gms **Lamb** – cut into cubes
1 **Bay Leaf**
1 teaspoon **Thyme**
1 teaspoon **Marjoram**
1 teaspoon **Rosemary**
1 teaspoon grated/ground **Nutmeg**
4 **Cloves**   6 tablespoons **Olive Oil**
1 teaspoon **Cayenne**   2 teaspoons of **Salt**
1 teaspoon **Coriander**   1 teaspoon of **Black Pepper**

Select a large pot for cooking that will be sufficient for all the ingredients, including the swollen rice when cooked. A 4-5 litre pot will be ample.

Cook the Puy Lentils as indicated in the 'Pusles' chapter by the conventional method, i.e. pot and lid. Discard the water and transfer the lentils into a suitable container for later use.

Heat the oil and fry the onion for about 3 minutes, stirring occasionally. Add the garlic and fry for another minute, stirring occasionally.

Add the Bay Leaf, Thyme, Marjoram, Rosemary, Nutmeg, Cloves, Cayenne, Coriander, salt, black pepper and fry for another minute to let the flavour of the spices infuse into the oil. Stir occasionally.

Add the lamb and continue to fry until the lamb is cooked. Stir occasionally to ensure the lamb is cooked all over.

Add the water, rice, Puy Lentils, tomatoes and green beans. Bring to the boil, reduce the heat on the cooker and simmer for about 8 minutes. Stir occasionally

Add the red pepper and simmer on a very low heat until the rice is cooked, stirring occasionally. The rice will soak up the water. If the water has evaporated before the rice is cooked, add small amounts of water to ensure the rice is cooked. Occasionally pinch the rice between two fingers to test if it is ready. It needs to be firm but soft, i.e. not gritty on the inside.

Green Lentils and Rice

Green Lentils and Rice

Serves 4 - (Time to prepare and cook = 1.5 hours)

160gms **Green Lentils**
80gms or half a cup of **Basmati Rice** per person
1 large **Onion** – chopped
4 cloves of **Garlic** – chopped
1.5 litres of hot water
150gms tinned **Sweet Corn**
150gms diced **Carrots**
150gms green **Capsicum Pepper** – cut into small pieces
300gms smoked **Gammon**
300gms cooked **Prawns**
3 teaspoons **Marjoram**
3 teaspoons **Thyme**
6 tablespoons **Corn Oil**
2 teaspoons of **Salt**
1 teaspoon of **Black Pepper**

Select a large pot for cooking that will be sufficient for all the ingredients, including the swollen rice when cooked. A 4-5 litre pot will be ample.

Boil the gammon in water for about half an hour until cooked. Cool and cut the gammon into small cubes.

Cook the Green Lentils as indicated in the 'Pusles' chapter by the conventional method, i.e. pot and lid. Discard the water and transfer the lentils into a suitable container for later use.

Heat the oil and fry the onion for about 3 minutes, stirring occasionally. Add the garlic and fry for another minute, stirring occasionally.

Add the Marjoram, Thyme, salt, black pepper and fry for another minute to let the flavour of the spices infuse into the oil. Stir occasionally.

Add the Green Lentils, gammon and 1 litre of water. Bring to the boil and reduce the heat on the cooker to simmer.

Add the rice, carrots and simmer for about 8 minutes. Stir occasionally.

Add the sweet corn, green pepper, prawns and continue to simmer on a very low heat until the rice is cooked. Stir occasionally. The rice will soak up the water. If the water has evaporated before the rice is cooked, add small amounts of water to ensure the rice is cooked. Occasionally pinch the rice between two fingers to test if it is ready. It needs to be firm but soft, i.e. not gritty on the inside.

Haricot Bean Rice

Haricot Bean Rice

Serves 4 - (Time to prepare and cook = 1.5 hours)

160gms **Haricot Beans** – soaked and cooked
80gms or half a cup of **Basmati Rice** per person
1 large **Onion** – chopped
4 cloves of **Garlic** – chopped
1.5 litres of hot water
400gms chopped tinned **Tomatoes**
150gms **Mushrooms** - chopped
150gms **Green Peas**
150gms red **Capsicum Pepper** – cut into small pieces
600gms **Lamb** – cut into cubes
3 teaspoons **Basil**
3 teaspoons **Thyme**   2 teaspoons of **Salt**
6 tablespoons **Corn Oil**   1 teaspoon of **Black Pepper**

Soak the Haricot Beans overnight in three times the amount of water to the volume of beans when cooking them by conventional cooking, i.e. not using a pressure cooker.

Select a large pot for cooking that will be sufficient for all the ingredients, including the swollen rice when cooked. A 4-5 litre pot will be ample.

Cook the Haricot Beans as indicated in the 'Pulses' chapter. The cooking time depends on whether a pot and lid (conventional) or a pressure cooker is used. The beans are cooked when they can be squashed between two fingers without them being too hard or too soft. Discard the water and transfer the beans into a suitable container for later use.

Heat the oil and fry the onion for about 3 minutes, stirring occasionally. Add the garlic and fry for another minute, stirring occasionally.

Add the Basil, Thyme, salt, black pepper and fry for another minute to let the flavour of the spices infuse into the oil. Stir occasionally.

Add the lamb and continue to fry until the lamb is cooked. Stir occasionally to ensure the lamb is cooked all over.

Add the water, rice, tomatoes, mushrooms, cooked beans, green peas and bring to the boil. Reduce the heat on the cooker and simmer for about 8 minutes.

Add the red pepper and simmer on a very low heat until the rice is cooked, stirring occasionally. The rice will soak up the water. If the water has evaporated before the rice is cooked, add small amounts of water to ensure the rice is cooked. Occasionally pinch the rice between two fingers to test if it is ready. It needs to be firm but soft, i.e. not gritty on the inside.

Green Lentils

Indian Green Lentils and Rice

Serves 4 - (Time to prepare and cook = 1 hour)

160gms **Green Lentils**
80gms or half a cup of **Basmati Rice** per person
1 large **Onion** – chopped
4 cloves of **Garlic** – chopped
1 litre of hot water
150gms **Mushrooms** - chopped
150gms red **Capsicum Pepper** – cut into small pieces
400ml can **Coconut Milk**, or grate, soak and squeeze the milk from one coconut
600gms **Chicken** – cut into cubes
1 tablespoon **Curry Powder**
6 tablespoons **Corn Oil**
2 teaspoons of **Salt**
1 teaspoon of **Black Pepper**

Select a large pot for cooking that will be sufficient for all the ingredients, including the swollen rice when cooked. A 4-5 litre pot will be ample.

Cook the Green Lentils as indicated in the 'Pusles' chapter by the conventional method, i.e. pot and lid. Discard the water and transfer the lentils into a suitable container for later use.

Heat the oil and fry the onion for about 3 minutes, stirring occasionally. Add the garlic and fry for another minute, stirring occasionally.

Add the Curry Powder, salt, black pepper and fry for another minute to let the flavour of the spices infuse into the oil. Stir occasionally.

Add the chicken and continue to fry until the chicken is cooked. Stir occasionally to ensure the chicken is cooked all over.

Add the Green Lentils, 1 litre of water and coconut milk. Bring to the boil and reduce the heat on the cooker to simmer.

Add the rice, mushrooms, red pepper and simmer on a very low heat until the rice is cooked, stirring occasionally. The rice will soak up the water and coconut milk. If the water has evaporated before the rice is cooked, add small amounts of water to ensure the rice is cooked. Occasionally pinch the rice between two fingers to test if it is ready. It needs to be firm but soft, i.e. not gritty on the inside.

Soya Beans

Indonesian Soya Bean Rice

Serves 4 - (Time to prepare and cook = 1 hour)

160gms **Soya Beans** – soaked and cooked
80gms or half a cup of **Basmati Rice** per person
1 large **Onion** – chopped
4 cloves of **Garlic** – chopped
1 litre of hot water
400gms chopped tinned **Tomatoes**
150gms tinned **Sweet Corn**
150gms green **Capsicum Pepper** – cut into small pieces
400ml can **Coconut Milk**, or grate, soak and squeeze the milk from one coconut
600gms **Chicken** – cut into cubes

1 tablespoon **Curry Powder**	2 teaspoons of **Salt**
6 tablespoons **Corn Oil**	1 teaspoon of **Black Pepper**

Soak the Soya Beans overnight in three times the amount of water to the volume of beans when cooking them by conventional cooking, i.e. not using a pressure cooker.

Select a large pot for cooking that will be sufficient for all the ingredients, including the swollen rice when cooked. A 4-5 litre pot will be ample.

Cook the Soya Beans as indicated in the 'Pulses' chapter. The cooking time depends on whether a pot and lid (conventional) or a pressure cooker is used. The beans are cooked when they can be squashed between two fingers without them being too hard or too soft. Discard the water and transfer the beans into a suitable container for later use.

Heat the oil and fry the onion for about 3 minutes, stirring occasionally. Add the garlic and fry for another minute, stirring occasionally.

Add the Curry Powder, salt, black pepper and fry for another minute to let the flavour of the spices infuse into the oil. Stir occasionally.

Add the chicken and continue to fry until the chicken is cooked. Stir occasionally to ensure the chicken is cooked all over.

Add the water, rice, cooked beans, tomatoes and coconut milk. Bring to the boil, reduce the heat on the cooker and simmer for about 8 minutes. Stir occasionally

Add the sweet corn, green pepper and simmer on a very low heat until the rice is cooked, stirring occasionally. The rice will soak up the water and coconut milk. If the water has evaporated before the rice is cooked, add small amounts of water to ensure the rice is cooked. Occasionally pinch the rice between two fingers to test if it is ready. It needs to be firm but soft, i.e. not gritty on the inside.

Borlotti Beans

Italian Borlotti Bean Rice

Serves 4 - (Time to prepare and cook = 1 hour)

160gms **Borlotti Beans** – soaked and cooked
80gms or half a cup of **Basmati Rice** per person
1 large **Onion** – chopped
4 cloves of **Garlic** – chopped
1.5 litres of hot water
400gms chopped tinned **Tomatoes**
150gms **Green Beans** – cut into small pieces
150gms diced **Carrots**
600gms **Lamb** – cut into cubes

1 teaspoon **Basil**	1 teaspoon **Oregano**
1 teaspoon **Marjoram**	1 teaspoon **Rosemary**
1 teaspoon **Paprika**	6 tablespoons **Olive Oil**
2 teaspoons of **Salt**	1 teaspoon of **Black Pepper**

Soak the Borlotti Beans overnight in three times the amount of water to the volume of beans when cooking them by conventional cooking, i.e. not using a pressure cooker.

Select a large pot for cooking that will be sufficient for all the ingredients, including the swollen rice when cooked. A 4-5 litre pot will be ample.

Cook the Borlotti Beans as indicated in the 'Pulses' chapter. The cooking time depends on whether a pot and lid (conventional) or a pressure cooker is used. The beans are cooked when they can be squashed between two fingers without them being too hard or too soft. Discard the water and transfer the beans into a suitable container for later use.

Heat the oil and fry the onion for about 3 minutes, stirring occasionally. Add the garlic and fry for another minute, stirring occasionally.

Add the Basil, Oregano, Marjoram, Rosemary, Paprika, salt, black pepper and fry for another minute to let the flavour of the spices infuse into the oil. Stir occasionally.

Add the lamb and continue to fry until the lamb is cooked. Stir occasionally to ensure the lamb is cooked all over.

Add the water and cooked beans. Bring to the boil and reduce the heat on the cooker to simmer.

Add the rice, tomatoes, green beans, carrots and simmer on a very low heat until the rice is cooked, stirring occasionally. The rice will soak up the water. If the water has evaporated before the rice is cooked, add small amounts of water to ensure the rice is cooked. Occasionally pinch the rice between two fingers to test if it is ready. It needs to be firm but soft, i.e. not gritty on the inside.

Cannellini Beans

Italian Cannellini Bean Rice

Serves 4 - (Time to prepare and cook = 1 hour)

160gms **Cannellini Beans** – soaked and cooked
80gms or half a cup of **Basmati Rice** per person
1 large **Onion** – chopped
4 cloves of **Garlic** – chopped
1 litre of hot water
400gms chopped tinned **Tomatoes**
150gms **Green Peas**
150gms tinned **Sweet Corn**
400ml can **Coconut Milk**, or grate, soak and squeeze the milk from one coconut
600gms cooked **Prawns**

1 teaspoon **Parsley**	1 teaspoon **Thyme**
1 teaspoon **Oregano**	1 teaspoon **Basil**
1 crushed **Bay Leaf**	3 teaspoons **Brown Sugar**
6 tablespoons **Olive Oil**	2 teaspoons of **Salt**

1 teaspoon of **Black Pepper**

Soak the Cannellini Beans overnight in three times the amount of water to the volume of beans when cooking them by conventional cooking, i.e. not using a pressure cooker.

Select a large pot for cooking that will be sufficient for all the ingredients, including the swollen rice when cooked. A 4-5 litre pot will be ample.

Cook the Cannellini Beans as indicated in the 'Pulses' chapter. The cooking time depends on whether a pot and lid (conventional) or a pressure cooker is used. The beans are cooked when they can be squashed between two fingers without them being too hard or too soft. Discard the water and transfer the beans into a suitable container for later use.

Heat the oil and fry the onion for about 3 minutes, stirring occasionally. Add the garlic and fry for another minute, stirring occasionally.

Add the Parsley, Thyme, Oregano, Basil, Bay Leaf, brown sugar, salt, black pepper and fry for another minute to let the flavour of the spices infuse into the oil. Stir occasionally.

Add the water, cooked beans, green peas, and coconut milk. Bring to the boil and reduce the heat on the cooker to simmer.

Add the rice, tomatoes and simmer for about 8 minutes. Stir occasionally.

Add the cooked prawns, sweet corn and continue to simmer on a very low heat until the rice is cooked. Stir occasionally. The rice will soak up the water and coconut milk. If the water has evaporated before the rice is cooked, add small amounts of water to ensure the rice is cooked. Occasionally pinch the rice between two fingers to test if it is ready. It needs to be firm but soft, i.e. not gritty on the inside.

Aduki Beans

Japanese Aduki Bean Rice

Serves 4 - (Time to prepare and cook = 1 hour)

160gms **Aduki Beans** – soaked and cooked
80gms or half a cup of **Basmati Rice** per person
1 large **Onion** – chopped
4 cloves of **Garlic** – chopped
1.5 litres of hot water
150gms **Mushrooms** - chopped
150gms diced **Carrots**
600gms cooked **Prawns**
3 teaspoons ground **Ginger**
4 teaspoons **Fish Sauce**
4 teaspoons **Soy Sauce**
3 tablespoons **Sesame Oil**
Salt to taste
1 teaspoon of **Black Pepper**

Soak the Aduki Beans overnight in three times the amount of water to the volume of beans when cooking them by conventional cooking, i.e. not using a pressure cooker.

Select a large pot for cooking that will be sufficient for all the ingredients, including the swollen rice when cooked. A 4-5 litre pot will be ample.

Cook the Aduki Beans as indicated in the 'Pulses' chapter. The cooking time depends on whether a pot and lid (conventional) or a pressure cooker is used. The beans are cooked when they can be squashed between two fingers without them being too hard or too soft. Discard the water and transfer the beans into a suitable container for later use.

Heat the oil and fry the onion for about 3 minutes, stirring occasionally. Add the garlic and fry for another minute, stirring occasionally.

Add the ground ginger, fish sauce,, black pepper and fry for another minute to let the flavour of the spices infuse into the oil. Stir occasionally.

Add the water and cooked beans. Bring to the boil and reduce the heat on the cooker to simmer.

Add the rice, mushrooms, carrots and simmer for about 8 minutes. Stir occasionally.

Add the cooked prawns and soy sauce. Add salt to taste. Continue to simmer on a very low heat until the rice is cooked. Stir occasionally. The rice will soak up the water. If the water has evaporated before the rice is cooked, add small amounts of water to ensure the rice is cooked. Occasionally pinch the rice between two fingers to test if it is ready. It needs to be firm but soft, i.e. not gritty on the inside.

Kidney Bean Rice

Kidney Bean Rice

Serves 4 - (Time to prepare and cook = 1 hour)

160gms **Red Kidney Beans** – soaked and cooked
80gms or half a cup of **Basmati Rice** per person
1 large **Onion** – chopped
4 cloves of **Garlic** – chopped
1.5 litres of hot water
150gms **Green Beans** – cut into small pieces
150gms tinned **Sweet Corn**
150gms red **Capsicum Pepper** – cut into small pieces
4 small **Chilli Peppers** – chopped or grounded
600gms **Beef** – cut into cubes (see variety of meats chapter)
3 teaspoons **Marjoram**
3 teaspoons **Basil**   2 teaspoons of **Salt**
6 tablespoons **Corn Oil**   1 teaspoon of **Black Pepper**

Soak the Kidney Beans overnight in three times the amount of water to the volume of beans when cooking them by conventional cooking, i.e. not using a pressure cooker.

Select a large pot for cooking that will be sufficient for all the ingredients, including the swollen rice when cooked. A 4-5 litre pot will be ample.

Cook the Kidney Beans as indicated in the 'Pulses' chapter. The cooking time depends on whether a pot and lid (conventional) or a pressure cooker is used. The beans are cooked when they can be squashed between two fingers without them being too hard or too soft. Discard the water and transfer the beans into a suitable container for later use.

Heat the oil and fry the onion for about 3 minutes, stirring occasionally. Add the garlic and fry for another minute, stirring occasionally.

Add the Marjoram, Basil, chilli peppers, salt, black pepper and fry for another minute to let the flavour of the spices infuse into the oil. Stir occasionally.

Add the beef and continue to fry until the beef is cooked. Stir occasionally to ensure the beef is cooked all over.

Add the water, cooked beans, rice, green beans and bring to the boil. Reduce the heat on the cooker and simmer for about 8 minutes, stirring occasionally.

Add the sweet corn, red pepper and simmer on a very low heat until the rice is cooked, stirring occasionally. The rice will soak up the water. If the water has evaporated before the rice is cooked, add small amounts of water to ensure the rice is cooked. Occasionally pinch the rice between two fingers to test if it is ready. It needs to be firm but soft, i.e. not gritty on the inside.

Split Peas

Latin Split Pea Rice

Serves 4 - (Time to prepare and cook = 1 hour)

160gms **Split Peas** – soaked and nearly cooked
80gms or half a cup of **Basmati Rice** per person
1 large **Onion** – chopped
4 cloves of **Garlic** – chopped
1.5 litres of hot water
150gms **Green Beans** – cut into small pieces
150gms **Mushrooms** - chopped
600gms **Chicken** – cut into cubes
1 teaspoon dry **Mustard Powder**
Zest of 1 **Orange**
1 teaspoon **Allspice**
1 teaspoon grated/ground **Nutmeg**
1 teaspoon ground **Ginger**
1 teaspoon **Cayenne**   6 tablespoons **Corn Oil**
2 teaspoons of **Salt**   1 teaspoon of **Black Pepper**

Soak the Split Peas for about 4 hours in three times the amount of water to the volume of peas.

Select a large pot for cooking that will be sufficient for all the ingredients, including the swollen rice when cooked. A 4-5 litre pot will be ample.

Cook the Split Peas as indicated in the 'Pulses' chapter. The cooking time depends on whether a pot and lid (conventional) or a pressure cooker is used. The peas are ready when you can squash them between two fingers without them being too hard or too soft. Discard the water and transfer the peas into a suitable container for later use.

Heat the oil and fry the onion for about 3 minutes, stirring occasionally. Add the garlic and fry for another minute, stirring occasionally.

Add the Mustard Powder, orange zest, Allspice, Nutmeg, ginger, Cayenne, salt, black pepper and fry for another minute to let the flavour of the spices infuse into the oil. Stir occasionally.

Add the chicken and continue to fry until the chicken is cooked. Stir occasionally to ensure the chicken is cooked all over.

Add the water and Split Peas. Bring to the boil and reduce the heat on the cooker to simmer.

Add the rice, green beans, mushrooms and simmer on a very low heat until the rice is cooked, stirring occasionally. The rice will soak up the water. If the water has evaporated before the rice is cooked, add small amounts of water to ensure the rice is cooked. Occasionally pinch the rice between two fingers to test if it is ready. It needs to be firm but soft, i.e. not gritty on the inside.

Butter Beans

Mediterranean Butter Bean Rice

Serves 4 - (Time to prepare and cook = 1 hour)

160gms **Butter Beans** – soaked and cooked
80gms or half a cup of **Basmati Rice** per person
1 large **Onion** – chopped
4 cloves of **Garlic** – chopped
1.5 litres of hot water
400gms chopped tinned **Tomatoes**
150gms **Green Beans** – cut into small pieces
150gms diced **Carrots**
600gms **Beef** – cut into cubes (see variety of meats chapter)
3 teaspoons **Coriander**
3 teaspoons **Oregano**
Juice from 1 **Lemon**   2 teaspoons of **Salt**
6 tablespoons **Olive Oil**   2 teaspoon of **Black Pepper**

Soak the Butter Beans overnight in three times the amount of water to the volume of beans when cooking them by conventional cooking, i.e. not using a pressure cooker.

Select a large pot for cooking that will be sufficient for all the ingredients, including the swollen rice when cooked. A 4-5 litre pot will be ample.

Cook the Butter Beans as indicated in the 'Pulses' chapter. The cooking time depends on whether a pot and lid (conventional) or a pressure cooker is used. The beans are cooked when they can be squashed between two fingers without them being too hard or too soft. Discard the water and transfer the beans into a suitable container for later use.

Heat the oil and fry the onion for about 3 minutes, stirring occasionally. Add the garlic and fry for another minute, stirring occasionally.

Add the Coriander, Oregano, lemon juice, salt, black pepper and fry for another minute to let the flavour of the spices infuse into the oil. Stir occasionally.

Add the beef and continue to fry until the beef is cooked. Stir occasionally to ensure the beef is cooked all over.

Add the water and cooked beans. Bring to the boil and reduce the heat on the cooker to simmer.

Add the rice, tomatoes, green beans, carrots and simmer on a very low heat until the rice is cooked, stirring occasionally. The rice will soak up the water. If the water has evaporated before the rice is cooked, add small amounts of water to ensure the rice is cooked. Occasionally pinch the rice between two fingers to test if it is ready. It needs to be firm but soft, i.e. not gritty on the inside.

Flageolet Beans

Mediterranean Flageolet Bean Rice

Serves 4 - (Time to prepare and cook = 1 hour)

160gms **Flageolet Beans** – soaked and cooked
80gms or half a cup of **Basmati Rice** per person
1 large **Onion** – chopped
4 cloves of **Garlic** – chopped
1.5 litres of hot water
400gms chopped tinned **Tomatoes**
150gms tinned **Sweet Corn**
150gms diced **Carrots**
600gms **Pork** – cut into cubes
3 teaspoons **Coriander**
3 teaspoons **Oregano**
Juice of 1 **Lemon**　　　　　　　　2 teaspoons of **Salt**
6 tablespoons **Olive Oil**　　　　　　1 teaspoon of **Black Pepper**

Soak the Flageolet Beans overnight in three times the amount of water to the volume of beans when cooking them by conventional cooking, i.e. not using a pressure cooker.

Select a large pot for cooking that will be sufficient for all the ingredients, including the swollen rice when cooked. A 4-5 litre pot will be ample.

Cook the Flageolet Beans as indicated in the 'Pulses' chapter. The cooking time depends on whether a pot and lid (conventional) or a pressure cooker is used. The beans are cooked when they can be squashed between two fingers without them being too hard or too soft. Discard the water and transfer the beans into a suitable container for later use.

Heat the oil and fry the onion for about 3 minutes, stirring occasionally. Add the garlic and fry for another minute, stirring occasionally.

Add the Coriander, Oregano, lemon juice, salt, black pepper and fry for another minute to let the flavour of the spices infuse into the oil. Stir occasionally.

Add the pork and continue to fry until the pork is cooked. Stir occasionally to ensure the pork is cooked all over.

Add the water, rice, cooked beans, tomatoes and carrots. Bring to the boil, reduce the heat on the cooker and simmer for about 8 minutes. Stir occasionally.

Add the sweet corn and simmer on a very low heat until the rice is cooked, stirring occasionally. The rice will soak up the water. If the water has evaporated before the rice is cooked, add small amounts of water to ensure the rice is cooked. Occasionally pinch the rice between two fingers to test if it is ready. It needs to be firm but soft, i.e. not gritty on the inside.

Kidney Beans

Mexican Kidney Bean Rice

Serves 4 - (Time to prepare and cook = 1 hour)

160gms **Red Kidney Beans** – soaked and cooked
80gms or half a cup of **Basmati Rice** per person
1 large **Onion** – chopped
4 cloves of **Garlic** – chopped
1.5 litres of hot water
150gms **Mushrooms** - chopped
150gms diced **Carrots**
600gms **Chicken** – cut into cubes
4 small **Chilli Peppers** – chopped or grounded
1 teaspoon **Paprika**
1 teaspoon **Coriander**
1 teaspoon **Parsley**
Zest of 1 **Lemon** and 1 **Orange**   2 teaspoons of **Salt**
6 tablespoons **Corn Oil**   1 teaspoon of **Black Pepper**

Soak the Kidney Beans overnight in three times the amount of water to the volume of beans when cooking them by conventional cooking, i.e. not using a pressure cooker.

Select a large pot for cooking that will be sufficient for all the ingredients, including the swollen rice when cooked. A 4-5 litre pot will be ample.

Cook the Kidney Beans as indicated in the 'Pulses' chapter. The cooking time depends on whether a pot and lid (conventional) or a pressure cooker is used. The beans are cooked when they can be squashed between two fingers without them being too hard or too soft. Discard the water and transfer the beans into a suitable container for later use.

Heat the oil and fry the onion for about 3 minutes, stirring occasionally. Add the garlic and fry for another minute, stirring occasionally.

Add the chilli peppers, Paprika, Coriander, Parsley, the lemon and orange zest, salt, black pepper and fry for another minute to let the flavour of the spices infuse into the oil. Stir occasionally.

Add the chicken and continue to fry until the chicken is cooked. Stir occasionally to ensure the chicken is cooked all over.

Add the water and cooked beans. Bring to the boil and reduce the heat on the cooker to simmer.

Add the rice, mushrooms, carrots and simmer on a very low heat until the rice is cooked, stirring occasionally. The rice will soak up the water. If the water has evaporated before the rice is cooked, add small amounts of water to ensure the rice is cooked. Occasionally pinch the rice between two fingers to test if it is ready. It needs to be firm but soft, i.e. not gritty on the inside.

Mung Bean Rice

Mung Bean Rice

Serves 4 - (Time to prepare and cook = 1 hour)

160gms **Mung Beans** – soaked and cooked
80gms or half a cup of **Basmati Rice** per person
1 large **Onion** – chopped
4 cloves of **Garlic** – chopped
1.5 litres of hot water
150gms tinned **Sweet Corn**
150gms diced **Carrots**
150gms green **Capsicum Pepper** – cut into small pieces
4 small **Chilli Peppers** – chopped or grounded
600gms **Pork** – cut into cubes
3 teaspoons **Marjoram**
3 teaspoons **Oregano**   2 teaspoons of **Salt**
6 tablespoons **Corn Oil**   1 teaspoon of **Black Pepper**

Soak the Mung Beans overnight in three times the amount of water to the volume of beans when cooking them by conventional cooking, i.e. not using a pressure cooker.

Select a large pot for cooking that will be sufficient for all the ingredients, including the swollen rice when cooked. A 4-5 litre pot will be ample.

Cook the Mung Beans as indicated in the 'Pulses' chapter. The cooking time depends on whether a pot and lid (conventional) or a pressure cooker is used. The beans are cooked when they can be squashed between two fingers without them being too hard or too soft. Discard the water and transfer the beans into a suitable container for later use.

Heat the oil and fry the onion for about 3 minutes, stirring occasionally. Add the garlic and fry for another minute, stirring occasionally.

Add the Marjoram, Oregano, chilli peppers, salt, black pepper and fry for another minute to let the flavour of the spices infuse into the oil. Stir occasionally.

Add the pork and continue to fry until the pork is cooked. Stir occasionally to ensure the pork is cooked all over.

Add the water, cooked beans, rice, carrots and bring to the boil. Reduce the heat on the cooker and simmer for about 8 minutes, stirring occasionally.

Add the sweet corn, green pepper and simmer on a very low heat until the rice is cooked, stirring occasionally. The rice will soak up the water. If the water has evaporated before the rice is cooked, add small amounts of water to ensure the rice is cooked. Occasionally pinch the rice between two fingers to test if it is ready. It needs to be firm but soft, i.e. not gritty on the inside.

Pigeon Pea Rice

Pigeon Pea Rice

Serves 4 - (Time to prepare and cook = 1 hour)

160gms **Pigeon Peas** – soaked and cooked
80gms or half a cup of **Basmati Rice** per person
1 large **Onion** – chopped
4 cloves of **Garlic** – chopped
1 litre of hot water
150gms **Mushrooms** - chopped
150gms tinned **Sweet Corn**
400ml can **Coconut Milk**, or grate, soak and squeeze the milk from one coconut
150gms red **Capsicum Pepper** – cut into small pieces
300gms **Chicken** – cut into cubes
300gms cooked **Prawns**
3 teaspoons **Basil**
3 teaspoons **Chives**   6 tablespoons **Corn Oil**
2 teaspoons of **Salt**   1 teaspoon of **Black Pepper**

Soak the Pigeon Peas overnight in three times the amount of water to the volume of peas.

Select a large pot for cooking that will be sufficient for all the ingredients, including the swollen rice when cooked. A 4-5 litre pot will be ample.

Cook the Pigeon Peas as indicated in the 'Pulses' chapter. The cooking time depends on whether a pot and lid (conventional) or a pressure cooker is used. The peas are cooked when they can be squashed between two fingers without them being too hard or too soft. Discard the water and transfer the peas into a suitable container for later use.

Heat the oil and fry the onion for about 3 minutes, stirring occasionally. Add the garlic and fry for another minute, stirring occasionally.

Add the Basil, Chives, salt, black pepper and fry for another minute to let the flavour of the spices infuse into the oil. Stir occasionally.

Add the chicken and continue to fry until the chicken is cooked. Stir occasionally to ensure the chicken is cooked all over.

Add the water, rice, cooked peas, mushrooms and coconut milk. Bring to the boil, reduce the heat on the cooker and simmer for about 8 minutes, stirring occasionally.

Add the cooked prawns, sweet corn, red pepper and continue to simmer on a very low heat until the rice is cooked. Stir occasionally. The rice will soak up the water and coconut milk. If the water has evaporated before the rice is cooked, add small amounts of water to ensure the rice is cooked. Occasionally pinch the rice between two fingers to test if it is ready. It needs to be firm but soft, i.e. not gritty on the inside.

Pinto Bean Rice

Pinto Bean Rice

Serves 4 - (Time to prepare and cook = 1 hour)

160gms **Pinto Beans** – soaked and cooked
80gms or half a cup of **Basmati Rice** per person
1 large **Onion** – chopped
4 cloves of **Garlic** – chopped
1.5 litres of hot water
400gms chopped tinned **Tomatoes**
150gms **Green Beans** – cut into small pieces
150gms tinned **Sweet Corn**
150gms red **Capsicum Pepper** – cut into small pieces
4 small **Chilli Peppers** – chopped or grounded
600gms **Lamb** – cut into cubes
3 teaspoons **Thyme**
3 teaspoons **Chives**   2 teaspoons of **Salt**
6 tablespoons **Corn Oil**   1 teaspoon of **Black Pepper**

Soak the Pinto Beans overnight in three times the amount of water to the volume of beans when cooking them by conventional cooking, i.e. not using a pressure cooker.

Select a large pot for cooking that will be sufficient for all the ingredients, including the swollen rice when cooked. A 4-5 litre pot will be ample.

Cook the Pinto Beans as indicated in the 'Pulses' chapter. The cooking time depends on whether a pot and lid (conventional) or a pressure cooker is used. The beans are cooked when they can be squashed between two fingers without them being too hard or too soft. Discard the water and transfer the beans into a suitable container for later use.

Heat the oil and fry the onion for about 3 minutes, stirring occasionally. Add the garlic and fry for another minute, stirring occasionally.

Add the Thyme, Chives, chilli peppers, salt, black pepper and fry for another minute to let the flavour of the spices infuse into the oil. Stir occasionally.

Add the lamb and continue to fry until the lamb is cooked. Stir occasionally to ensure the lamb is cooked all over.

Add the water, cooked beans, rice, green beans, tomatoes and bring to the boil. Reduce the heat on the cooker and simmer for about 8 minutes, stirring occasionally.

Add the sweet corn, red pepper and simmer on a very low heat until the rice is cooked, stirring occasionally. The rice will soak up the water. If the water has evaporated before the rice is cooked, add small amounts of water to ensure the rice is cooked. Occasionally pinch the rice between two fingers to test if it is ready. It needs to be firm but soft, i.e. not gritty on the inside.

Puy Lentils and Rice

Puy Lentils and Rice

Serves 4 - (Time to prepare and cook = 1 hour)

160gms **Puy Lentils**
80gms or half a cup of **Basmati Rice** per person
1 large **Onion** – chopped
4 cloves of **Garlic** – chopped
1 litre of hot water
150gms tinned **Sweet Corn**
150gms diced **Carrots**
400ml can **Coconut Milk**, or grate, soak and squeeze the milk from one coconut
150gms red **Capsicum Pepper** – cut into small pieces
600gms **Chicken** – cut into cubes
3 teaspoons **Basil**
3 teaspoons **Oregano**
6 tablespoons **Corn Oil**
2 teaspoons of **Salt**
1 teaspoon of **Black Pepper**

Select a large pot for cooking that will be sufficient for all the ingredients, including the swollen rice when cooked. A 4-5 litre pot will be ample.

Cook the Puy Lentils as indicated in the 'Pusles' chapter by the conventional method, i.e. pot and lid. Discard the water and transfer the lentils into a suitable container for later use.

Heat the oil and fry the onion for about 3 minutes, stirring occasionally. Add the garlic and fry for another minute, stirring occasionally.

Add the Basil, Oregano, salt, black pepper and fry for another minute to let the flavour of the spices infuse into the oil. Stir occasionally.

Add the chicken and continue to fry until the chicken is cooked. Stir occasionally to ensure the chicken is cooked all over.

Add the water, rice, Puy Lentils, carrots and coconut milk. Bring to the boil and reduce the heat on the cooker to simmer.

Add the sweet corn, red pepper and simmer on a very low heat until the rice is cooked, stirring occasionally. The rice will soak up the water and coconut milk. If the water has evaporated before the rice is cooked, add small amounts of water to ensure the rice is cooked. Occasionally pinch the rice between two fingers to test if it is ready. It needs to be firm but soft, i.e. not gritty on the inside.

Red Lentils and Rice

Red Lentils and Rice

Serves 4 - (Time to prepare and cook = 1 hour)

160gms **Red Lentils**
80gms or half a cup of **Basmati Rice** per person
1 large **Onion** – chopped
4 cloves of **Garlic** – chopped
1 litre of hot water
150gms **Mushrooms** - chopped
150gms **Green Peas**
400ml can **Coconut Milk**, or grate, soak and squeeze the milk from one coconut
150gms red **Capsicum Pepper** – cut into small pieces
300gms **Chicken** – cut into cubes
300gms cooked **Prawns**
3 teaspoons **Thyme**
3 teaspoons **Chives**
6 tablespoons **Corn Oil**
2 teaspoons of **Salt**
1 teaspoon of **Black Pepper**

Select a large pot for cooking that will be sufficient for all the ingredients, including the swollen rice when cooked. A 4-5 litre pot will be ample.

The Red Lentils do not need to be cooked beforehand and will be added to the dish as described below.

Heat the oil and fry the onion for about 3 minutes, stirring occasionally. Add the garlic and fry for another minute, stirring occasionally.

Add the Thyme, Chives, salt, black pepper and fry for another minute to let the flavour of the spices infuse into the oil. Stir occasionally.

Add the chicken and continue to fry until the chicken is cooked. Stir occasionally to ensure the chicken is cooked all over.

Add the water, rice, Red Lentils, green peas, mushrooms and coconut milk. Bring to the boil, reduce the heat on the cooker and simmer for about 8 minutes, stir occasionally.

Add the cooked prawns, red pepper and continue to simmer on a very low heat until the rice is cooked. Stir occasionally. The rice will soak up the water and coconut milk. If the water has evaporated before the rice is cooked, add small amounts of water to ensure the rice is cooked. Occasionally pinch the rice between two fingers to test if it is ready. It needs to be firm but soft, i.e. not gritty on the inside.

Broad Beans

South American Broad Bean Rice

Serves 4 - (Time to prepare and cook = 1 hour)

160gms Broad **Beans** – fresh and cooked
80gms or half a cup of **Basmati Rice** per person
1 large **Onion** – chopped
4 cloves of **Garlic** – chopped
1 litre of hot water
150gms tinned **Sweet Corn**
150gms red **Capsicum Pepper** – cut into small pieces
400ml can **Coconut Milk**, or grate, soak and squeeze the milk from one coconut
600gms **Lamb** – cut into cubes
4 small **Chilli Peppers** – chopped or grounded
1 teaspoon **Paprika**
1 teaspoon ground **Cumin**
1 teaspoon **Oregano**   2 teaspoons of **Salt**
6 tablespoons **Corn Oil**   1 teaspoon of **Black Pepper**

Select a large pot for cooking that will be sufficient for all the ingredients, including the swollen rice when cooked. A 4-5 litre pot will be ample.

Cook the fresh Broad Beans as indicated in the 'Pulses' chapter. As the beans are fresh, they should be cooked by conventional means, i.e. pot and lid. The beans are cooked when they can be squashed between two fingers without them being too hard or too soft. Discard the water and transfer the beans into a suitable container for later use.

Heat the oil and fry the onion for about 3 minutes, stirring occasionally. Add the garlic and fry for another minute, stirring occasionally.

Add the chilli peppers, Paprika, ground Cumin, Oregano, salt, black pepper and fry for another minute to let the flavour of the spices infuse into the oil. Stir occasionally.

Add the lamb and continue to fry until the lamb is cooked. Stir occasionally to ensure the lamb is cooked all over.

Add the water, rice, cooked beans and coconut milk. Bring to the boil, reduce the heat on the cooker and simmer for about 8 minutes. Stir occasionally.

Add the sweet corn, red pepper and simmer on a very low heat until the rice is cooked, stirring occasionally. The rice will soak up the water and coconut milk. If the water has evaporated before the rice is cooked, add small amounts of water to ensure the rice is cooked. Occasionally pinch the rice between two fingers to test if it is ready. It needs to be firm but soft, i.e. not gritty on the inside.

Soya Bean Rice

Soya Bean Rice

Serves 4 - (Time to prepare and cook = 1.5 hours)

160gms **Soya Beans** – soaked and cooked
80gms or half a cup of **Basmati Rice** per person
1 large **Onion** – chopped
4 cloves of **Garlic** – chopped
1.5 litres of hot water
400gms chopped tinned **Tomatoes**
150gms **Green Beans** – cut into small pieces
150gms **Mushrooms** - chopped
150gms red **Capsicum Pepper** – cut into small pieces
300gms smoked **Gammon**
300gms cooked **Prawns**
3 teaspoons **Marjoram**
3 teaspoons **Chives**   6 tablespoons **Corn Oil**
2 teaspoons of **Salt**   1 teaspoon of **Black Pepper**

Soak the Soya Beans overnight in three times the amount of water to the volume of beans when cooking them by conventional cooking, i.e. not using a pressure cooker.

Select a large pot for cooking that will be sufficient for all the ingredients, including the swollen rice when cooked. A 4-5 litre pot will be ample.

Boil the gammon in water for about half an hour until cooked. Cool and cut the gammon into small cubes.

Cook the Soya Beans as indicated in the 'Pulses' chapter. The cooking time depends on whether a pot and lid (conventional) or a pressure cooker is used. The beans are cooked when they can be squashed between two fingers without them being too hard or too soft. Discard the water and transfer the beans into a suitable container for later use.

Heat the oil and fry the onion for about 3 minutes, stirring occasionally. Add the garlic and fry for another minute, stirring occasionally.

Add the Marjoram, Chives, salt, black pepper and fry for another minute to let the flavour of the spices infuse into the oil. Stir occasionally.

Add the water, rice, cooked beans, tomatoes, green beans, mushrooms and gammon. Bring to the boil, reduce the heat on the cooker and simmer for about 8 minutes, stirring occasionally.

Add the prawns and red pepper, and continue to simmer on a very low heat until the rice is cooked. Stir occasionally. The rice will soak up the water. If the water has evaporated before the rice is cooked, add small amounts of water to ensure the rice is cooked. Occasionally pinch the rice between two fingers to test if it is ready. It needs to be firm but soft, i.e. not gritty on the inside.

Pinto Beans

Spanish Pinto Bean Rice

Serves 4 - (Time to prepare and cook = 1 hour)

160gms **Pinto Beans** – soaked and cooked
80gms or half a cup of **Basmati Rice** per person
1 large **Onion** – chopped
4 cloves of **Garlic** – chopped
1.5 litres of hot water
150gms **Green Peas**
150gms red **Capsicum Pepper** – cut into small pieces
600gms **Chicken** – cut into cubes
1 teaspoon ground **Cumin**
1 teaspoon **Coriander**
1 teaspoon **Paprika**
Zest of 1 **Lemon** and 1 **Orange**   2 teaspoons of **Salt**
6 tablespoons **Corn Oil**   1 teaspoon of **Black Pepper**

Soak the Pinto Beans overnight in three times the amount of water to the volume of beans when cooking them by conventional cooking, i.e. not using a pressure cooker.

Select a large pot for cooking that will be sufficient for all the ingredients, including the swollen rice when cooked. A 4-5 litre pot will be ample.

Cook the Pinto Beans as indicated in the 'Pulses' chapter. The cooking time depends on whether a pot and lid (conventional) or a pressure cooker is used. The beans are cooked when they can be squashed between two fingers without them being too hard or too soft. Discard the water and transfer the beans into a suitable container for later use.

Heat the oil and fry the onion for about 3 minutes, stirring occasionally. Add the garlic and fry for another minute, stirring occasionally.

Add the ground Cumin, Coriander, Paprika, the lemon and orange zest, salt, black pepper and fry for another minute to let the flavour of the spices infuse into the oil. Stir occasionally.

Add the chicken and continue to fry until the chicken is cooked. Stir occasionally to ensure the chicken is cooked all over.

Add the water, rice, cooked beans and green peas. Bring to the boil, reduce the heat on the cooker and simmer for about 8 minutes. Stir occasionally

Add the red pepper and simmer on a very low heat until the rice is cooked, stirring occasionally. The rice will soak up the water. If the water has evaporated before the rice is cooked, add small amounts of water to ensure the rice is cooked. Occasionally pinch the rice between two fingers to test if it is ready. It needs to be firm but soft, i.e. not gritty on the inside.

Split Pea Rice

Split Pea Rice

Serves 4 - (Time to prepare and cook = 1 hour)

160gms **Split Peas** – soaked and nearly cooked
80gms or half a cup of **Basmati Rice** per person
1 large **Onion** – chopped
4 cloves of **Garlic** – chopped
1 litre of hot water
400ml can **Coconut Milk**, or grate, soak and squeeze the milk from one coconut
150gms red **Capsicum Pepper** – cut into small pieces
4 small **Chilli Peppers** – chopped or grounded
600gms cooked **Prawns**
3 teaspoons **Basil**
3 teaspoons **Chives**
4 tablespoons **Corn Oil**
2 teaspoons of **Salt**
1 teaspoon of **Black Pepper**

Soak the Split Peas for about 4 hours in three times the amount of water to the volume of peas.

Select a large pot for cooking that will be sufficient for all the ingredients, including the swollen rice when cooked. A 4-5 litre pot will be ample.

Cook the Split Peas as indicated in the 'Pulses' chapter. The cooking time depends on whether a pot and lid (conventional) or a pressure cooker is used. The peas are ready when you can squash them between two fingers without them being too hard or too soft. Discard the water and transfer the peas into a suitable container for later use.

Heat the oil and fry the onion for about 3 minutes, stirring occasionally. Add the garlic and fry for another minute, stirring occasionally.

Add the Basil, Chives, chilli peppers, salt, black pepper and fry for another minute to let the flavour of the spices infuse into the oil. Stir occasionally.

Add the water, rice, cooked Split Peas and coconut milk. Bring to the boil, reduce the heat on the cooker and simmer for about 8 minutes, stirring occasionally.

Add the cooked prawns, red pepper and continue to simmer on a very low heat until the rice is cooked. Stir occasionally. The rice will soak up the water and coconut milk. If the water has evaporated before the rice is cooked, add small amounts of water to ensure the rice is cooked. Occasionally pinch the rice between two fingers to test if it is ready. It needs to be firm but soft, i.e. not gritty on the inside.

Chick Peas

Sri Lankan Chick Pea Rice

Serves 4 - (Time to prepare and cook = 1 hour)

160gms **Chick Peas** – soaked and cooked
80gms or half a cup of **Basmati Rice** per person
1 large **Onion** – chopped
4 cloves of **Garlic** – chopped
1.5 litres of hot water
400gms chopped tinned **Tomatoes**
150gms **Green Beans** – cut into small pieces
150gms **Mushrooms** - chopped
600gms **Beef** – cut into cubes (see variety of meats chapter)
1 tablespoon **Curry Powder**
6 tablespoons **Corn Oil**
2 teaspoons of **Salt**
1 teaspoon of **Black Pepper**

Soak the Chick Peas overnight in three times the amount of water to the volume of peas.

Select a large pot for cooking that will be sufficient for all the ingredients, including the swollen rice when cooked. A 4-5 litre pot will be ample.

Cook the Chick Peas as indicated in the 'Pulses' chapter. The cooking time depends on whether a pot and lid (conventional) or a pressure cooker is used. The peas are cooked when they can be squashed between two fingers without them being too hard or too soft. Discard the water and transfer the peas into a suitable container for later use.

Heat the oil and fry the onion for about 3 minutes, stirring occasionally. Add the garlic and fry for another minute, stirring occasionally.

Add the Curry Powder, salt, black pepper and fry for another minute to let the flavour of the spices infuse into the oil. Stir occasionally.

Add the beef and continue to fry until the beef is cooked. Stir occasionally to ensure the beef is cooked all over.

Add the water and cooked peas. Bring to the boil and reduce the heat on the cooker to simmer.

Add the rice, tomatoes, green beans, mushrooms and simmer on a very low heat until the rice is cooked, stirring occasionally. The rice will soak up the water. If the water has evaporated before the rice is cooked, add small amounts of water to ensure the rice is cooked. Occasionally pinch the rice between two fingers to test if it is ready. It needs to be firm but soft, i.e. not gritty on the inside.

Red Lentils

Thai Red Lentils and Rice

Serves 4 - (Time to prepare and cook = 1 hour)

160gms **Red Lentils**
80gms or half a cup of **Basmati Rice** per person
1 large **Onion** – chopped
4 cloves of **Garlic** – chopped
1 litre of hot water
150gms **Green Beans** – cut into small pieces
150gms **Mushrooms** - chopped
400ml can **Coconut Milk**, or grate, soak and squeeze the milk from one coconut
600gms **Pork** – cut into cubes
4 small **Chilli Peppers** – chopped or grounded
4 teaspoons **Soy Sauce**
Juice of 1 **Lime**
2 teaspoons ground **Ginger**
2 teaspoons **Coriander**
6 tablespoons **Sesame Oil**
2 teaspoons of **Salt**
1 teaspoon of **Black Pepper**

Select a large pot for cooking that will be sufficient for all the ingredients, including the swollen rice when cooked. A 4-5 litre pot will be ample.

The Red Lentils do not need to be cooked beforehand and will be added to the dish as described below.

Heat the oil and fry the onion for about 3 minutes, stirring occasionally. Add the garlic and fry for another minute, stirring occasionally.

Add the chilli peppers, soy sauce, lime juice, ground ginger, Coriander, salt, black pepper and fry for another minute to let the flavour of the spices infuse into the oil. Stir occasionally.

Add the pork and continue to fry until the pork is cooked. Stir occasionally to ensure the pork is cooked all over.

Add the water, Red Lentils and coconut milk. Bring to the boil and reduce the heat on the cooker to simmer.

Add the rice, green beans, mushrooms and simmer on a very low heat until the rice is cooked, stirring occasionally. The rice will soak up the water and coconut milk. If the water has evaporated before the rice is cooked, add small amounts of water to ensure the rice is cooked. Occasionally pinch the rice between two fingers to test if it is ready. It needs to be firm but soft, i.e. not gritty on the inside.

Black Eye Beans

West Indian Black Eye Bean Rice

Serves 4 - (Time to prepare and cook = 1 hour)

160gms **Black Eye Beans** – soaked and cooked
80gms or half a cup of **Basmati Rice** per person
1 large **Onion** – chopped
4 cloves of **Garlic** – chopped
1 litre of hot water
400gms chopped tinned **Tomatoes**
150gms **Mushrooms** - chopped
150gms **Green Peas**
400ml can **Coconut Milk**, or grate, soak and squeeze the milk from one coconut
600gms **Chicken** – cut into cubes

1 tablespoon **Curry Powder**	2 teaspoons of **Salt**
6 tablespoons **Corn Oil**	1 teaspoon of **Black Pepper**

Soak the Black Eye Beans overnight in three times the amount of water to the volume of beans when cooking them by conventional cooking, i.e. not using a pressure cooker.

Select a large pot for cooking that will be sufficient for all the ingredients, including the swollen rice when cooked. A 4-5 litre pot will be ample.

Cook the Black Eye Beans as indicated in the 'Pulses' chapter. The cooking time depends on whether a pot and lid (conventional) or a pressure cooker is used. The beans are cooked when they can be squashed between two fingers without them being too hard or too soft. Discard the water and transfer the beans into a suitable container for later use.

Heat the oil and fry the onion for about 3 minutes, stirring occasionally. Add the garlic and fry for another minute, stirring occasionally.

Add the Curry Powder, salt, black pepper and fry for another minute to let the flavour of the spices infuse into the oil. Stir occasionally.

Add the chicken and continue to fry until the chicken is cooked. Stir occasionally to ensure the chicken is cooked all over.

Add the water, cooked beans, green peas and coconut milk. Bring to the boil and reduce the heat on the cooker to simmer.

Add the rice, tomatoes, mushrooms and simmer on a very low heat until the rice is cooked, stirring occasionally. The rice will soak up the water and coconut milk. If the water has evaporated before the rice is cooked, add small amounts of water to ensure the rice is cooked. Occasionally pinch the rice between two fingers to test if it is ready. It needs to be firm but soft, i.e. not gritty on the inside.

Pigeon Peas

West Indian Pigeon Pea Rice

Serves 4 - (Time to prepare and cook = 1 hour)

160gms **Pigeon Peas** – soaked and cooked
80gms or half a cup of **Basmati Rice** per person
1 large **Onion** – chopped
4 cloves of **Garlic** – chopped
1 litre of hot water
400gms chopped tinned **Tomatoes**
150gms diced **Carrots**
150gms red **Capsicum Pepper** – cut into small pieces
400ml can **Coconut Milk**, or grate, soak and squeeze the milk from one coconut
600gms cooked **Prawns**
1 tablespoon **Curry Powder**
3 tablespoons **Corn Oil**
2 teaspoons of **Salt**
1 teaspoon of **Black Pepper**

Soak the Pigeon Peas overnight in three times the amount of water to the volume of peas.

Select a large pot for cooking that will be sufficient for all the ingredients, including the swollen rice when cooked. A 4-5 litre pot will be ample.

Cook the Pigeon Peas as indicated in the 'Pulses' chapter. The cooking time depends on whether a pot and lid (conventional) or a pressure cooker is used. The peas are cooked when they can be squashed between two fingers without them being too hard or too soft. Discard the water and transfer the peas into a suitable container for later use.

Heat the oil and fry the onion for about 3 minutes, stirring occasionally. Add the garlic and fry for another minute, stirring occasionally.

Add the Curry Powder, salt, black pepper and fry for another minute to let the flavour of the spices infuse into the oil. Stir occasionally.

Add the water, rice, cooked peas, tomatoes, carrots and coconut milk. Bring to the boil, reduce the heat on the cooker and simmer for about 8 minutes. Stir occasionally.

Add the cooked prawns, red pepper and continue to simmer on a very low heat until the rice is cooked. Stir occasionally. The rice will soak up the water and coconut milk. If the water has evaporated before the rice is cooked, add small amounts of water to ensure the rice is cooked. Occasionally pinch the rice between two fingers to test if it is ready. It needs to be firm but soft, i.e. not gritty on the inside.

Do It Yourself Recipes

This section allows the creation of your own dishes and the selection of your choice ingredients. That is the beauty about cooking, flexibility.

a) Beans

First of all, decide on the beans to use. Beans will be one of the ingredients that give the dish its main flavour. Refer to the **'Pulses'** chapter to select the beans.

Use about 40gms of beans per person, more or less can be used as desired. Remember to allow time to soak the beans, normally overnight or 12 hours. Ensure there is enough water in the container in which to soak the beans, as they will expand. As a rule, allow three times the volume of water to the volume of beans. Soaking is only required when cooking the beans by conventional method, i.e. not using a pressure cooker.

Always cook the beans as indicated in the **'Pulses'** chapter. Refer to the table in the chapter for cooking times. Discard the water after cooking the beans.

b) Rice

Refer to the **'Rice'** chapter to select the rice of your choice. **Allow about 80gms or half a cup of rice per person**. This of course depends on your hunger.

Remember the following:

Brown Rice or **Wild Rice** will take longer to cook than other rice. They may also be harder in texture.

The soft rice like **Jasmine Rice**, **Glutinous Rice** and **Japanese Rice** may be too soft and sticky.

Basmati Rice, **Long Grain Rice**, **Medium Grain Rice** and **Short Grain Rice** are most suitable for these types of rice dishes.

c) Meats

The word 'meats' is used as a generic term for **Sausages**, **Lamb**, **Pork**, **Beef**, **Chicken** and **Prawns** and **Gammon**.

Vegetarians - Do not despair. Meats do not have to be added to the dish. They will add some flavour to the dish but the dish will have the taste of the other ingredients, which also gives flavour to the dish.

Refer to the **'Meats'** chapter to select the meats to include in the dish. The important thing is that one, two or more meats can be used in each dish. A combination of meats will also give added flavour to the dish. It is your choice. The mixing of meats and prawns is ideal for a combination of land and surf tastes.

Use about 150gms of meat per person cut into cubes.

d) Onions and Garlic

Refer to the **'Onions'** and **'Garlic'** chapters. **Use one large onion and four cloves of garlic for every 4 people**.

Yellow Onions are best to use but for a change, why not use the red or white onion.

The garlic chapter shows different forms of garlic. Fresh garlic is best used but granulated, flaked or powdered garlic can be used instead. Again, it is your choice.

The fresh onion and garlic both need to be chopped.

e) Tomatoes

Tomatoes add taste and colour to any dish, although not mandatory for these rich dishes. If a bean is chosen that has a bland colour, like **Haricot Beans**, then adding tomatoes will give life to the dish.

The tomatoes should be chopped and I prefer to use chopped tinned tomatoes. **One tin (400gms) or six chopped tomatoes should be used for every 4-6 people**.

Refer to **'Vegetables'** chapter.

f) Vegetables

Try to use two or possibly three vegetables in each dish. They will give colour and most will add a sweet flavour to the dish.

Refer to the **'Vegetables'** chapter to make a choice from the preferred vegetables list. However, why not chose your own vegetables. Bear in mind that soft vegetables will dissolve, possibly to nothing, when cooked in these rice dishes.

Capsicum Peppers are ideal to use with two other vegetables. Capsicums will keep their colour when cooked which helps to make the dish look attractive. This is very important for presentation purposes.

Use about 100-150gms of mixed vegetables per person.

g) Spices

Spices will add that extra "oomph" or "je ne sais quoi" to any dish. The ones described in the **'Spices'** chapter are most suitable for cooking these rice dishes. Again, any spice of your choice can be used. Try combining different spices to see what flavours are achieved.

Use a combination of two spices. **Allow 3 teaspoons of each spice for every 4 people**.

h) Coconut

The coconut is a very versatile food item. Did you know that milk, water and oil come from the coconut. This however, is not the book to enthuse about the coconut, as it would take too long to describe its uses. Nevertheless, for the purpose of this cooking, the following is required from the coconut.

First of all, the coconut has a strong taste and will drastically change the flavour of any dish. Secondly, if you use grated coconut, this will alter the texture of the dish.

Coconut comes in different forms and for these dishes the milk from tinned **Coconut Milk** (400ml), a block of **Creamed Coconut** (only use 50gms) or the coconut itself is used.

If using a mature coconut, crack open the coconut and prise out the hard coconut flesh. The water that comes from the coconut is NOT the milk, as many people believe. Grate the coconut flesh into fine pieces and soak in 2 cups of hot water for about an hour. Pummel and squeeze the coconut mixture with your hands until the water turns very milky. The result is the coconut milk. Strain the milk off into a container.

Use about 400ml of Coconut Milk or 50gms of Creamed Coconut for every 4 people.

i) Chilli Peppers

Use fresh chillies, dried chillies or chilli powder according to your taste. Chilli Peppers will make food hot and pungent. They do bring out some flavours, but too much Chilli Peppers will temporarily damage the taste buds and the flavours of the dish will not be savoured.

As a rule use 4 or 5 small Chilli Peppers chopped or grounded for every 4 people.

j) Cooking the Dish

Now that all the ingredients ready, the dish can be cooked. The method of cooking is called a 'one pot' dish because, in theory, only one pot is required to cook these rice dishes. This saves on the washing up as well. Choose a pot that will be sufficient for all the ingredients, including the swollen rice when cooked.

The chosen beans should be soaked overnight so that they will be swollen by the absorption of the water. Using the pot, cook the beans in the water according to the times in the **'Pulses'** chapter. Extra water may need to be added during cooking. The beans are cooked when they can be squashed between two fingers without them being too hard or too soft. Discard the water and transfer the beans into a suitable container for later use.

Using 6 tablespoons of oil for every 4 people, heat the oil and sweat the chopped **Onions** for about 3 minutes, stirring occasionally. **Vegetable Oil**, **Olive Oil** or **Corn Oil** can be used.

Add the chopped **Garlic** and fry for another minute, stirring occasionally.

Add the spices and **Chilli Peppers** (if required) and fry for another minute to let the flavour of the spices infuse into the oil. Stir occasionally.

If pre-cooked meats are chosen they can be added later, e.g. **Gammon**, cooked **Prawns** or left over meats.

Add uncooked meats to the pot and continue frying until cooked, stirring occasionally. **Chicken** especially needs to be cooked thoroughly.

Add the water, cooked beans, **Tomatoes** (if required) and **Coconut Milk** (if required) to the pot and bring to the boil. Reduce the heat on the cooker to simmer.

Add salt and black pepper to taste. As a rule, use 2 teaspoons of salt and one teaspoon of black pepper for every 4 people.

Add the rice and vegetables and simmer on a very low heat until the rice is cooked, stirring occasionally. Pinch the rice between two fingers to test if it is ready. It needs to be firm but soft, i.e. not gritty on the inside. If the water has evaporated before the rice is cooked, add small amounts of water to ensure the rice is cooked.

A few tips to remember:-

Try not to burn the food at the bottom of the pot, hence the stirring.

Add extra hot water if the rice has absorbed the water and is still uncooked.

Do not add too much water. It is easier to put more in than take it out. If too much water is put in, the rice will be overcooked and stodgy.

The ideal consistency is where the dish is still a bit moist.

Excluding the cooking of the beans, the dish should take about half an hour to cook.

Serve with a garnish.

Index

A

Aduki Beans, 9, 25, 66, 67
Adzuki Beans, 9
Allspice, 16, 71
Alubia Beans, 9, 27, 31
Arborio Rice, 7, 8
Azuki Beans, 9

B

Basil, 16, 27, 31, 51, 57, 63, 65, 69, 81, 85, 95
Basmati Rice, 5, 7, 8, 23, 25, 27, 29, 31, 33, 35, 37, 39, 41, 43, 45, 47, 49, 51, 53, 55, 57, 59, 61, 63, 65, 67, 69, 71, 73, 75, 77, 79, 81, 83, 85, 87, 89, 91, 93, 95, 97, 99, 101, 103, 104
Bay Leaf, 16, 53, 65
Beef, 5, 17, 37, 39, 69, 73, 97, 104
Black Beans, 9, 10, 12, 13, 33, 46, 47
Black Eye Beans, 10, 35, 100, 101
Black Pepper, 16, 25, 27, 29, 31, 33, 35, 37, 39, 41, 43, 45, 47, 49, 51, 55, 57, 59, 61, 63, 65, 67, 69, 71, 73, 75, 77, 79, 81, 83, 85, 87, 89, 91, 93, 95, 97, 99, 101, 103
Black Turtle Beans, 10
Borlotti Beans, 10, 12, 13, 37, 62, 63
Botan Rice, 7, 8
Broad Beans, 10
Brown Rice, 7, 8, 104
Brown Sugar, 19, 29, 65
Butter Beans, 10, 11, 13, 41, 72, 73

C

Calrose Rice, 8
Cannellini Beans, 9, 10, 11, 13, 43, 64, 65
Capsicum Pepper, 16, 18, 25, 27, 33, 35, 37, 39, 41, 43, 45, 49, 51, 53, 55, 57, 59, 61, 69, 79, 81, 83, 85, 87, 89, 91, 93, 95, 103, 105
Capsicum Peppers, 16, 18, 105
Carrots, 18, 31, 33, 55, 63, 67, 73, 75, 77, 79, 85, 103
Cayenne, 16, 29, 53, 71
Chick Peas, 10, 11, 45, 96, 97
Chicken, 5, 17, 25, 45, 47, 51, 59, 61, 71, 77, 81, 85, 87, 93, 101, 104, 107
Chilli Peppers, 16, 35, 45, 69, 77, 79, 83, 89, 95, 99, 106
Chinese Five Spice, 16, 47, 49
Chinese Sweet Rice, 7, 8
Chives, 15, 16, 25, 39, 43, 81, 83, 87, 91, 95
Chops, 17
Chorizo Sausage, 17, 27, 41
Christmas Beans, 10
Chump Chops, 17
Cloves, 16, 53
Coconut Milk, 19, 25, 35, 45, 51, 59, 61, 65, 81, 85, 87, 89, 95, 99, 101, 103, 106, 107
Conventional Onions, 14
Coriander, 16, 53, 63, 73, 75, 77, 93, 99
Corn Oil, 19, 25, 27, 31, 33, 35, 37, 39, 41, 43, 45, 51, 55, 57, 59, 61, 69, 71, 77, 79, 81, 85, 87, 89, 91, 93, 95, 97, 101, 103, 106
Cranberry Beans, 10

Creamed Coconut, 106
Cumin, 16, 29, 89, 93
Curry Powder, 16, 59, 61, 97, 101, 103

D

Demerara Sugar, 19

E

English Beans, 10

F

Fava Beans, 11
Fayot Beans, 11
Fazolia Beans, 11
Fish Sauce, 19, 67
Flageolet Beans, 11, 51, 74, 75

G

Gammon, 5, 17, 35, 43, 45, 55, 91, 104, 106
Garbanzo Beans, 10, 11
Garlic, 5, 6, 15, 16, 18, 25, 27, 29, 31, 33, 35, 37, 39, 41, 43, 45, 47, 49, 51, 53, 55, 57, 59, 61, 63, 65, 67, 69, 71, 73, 75, 77, 79, 81, 83, 85, 87, 89, 91, 93, 95, 97, 99, 101, 103, 105, 106
Ginger, 16, 67, 71, 99
Glutinous Rice, 7, 8, 104
Green Beans, 18, 25, 27, 29, 39, 43, 47, 51, 53, 63, 69, 71, 73, 83, 91, 97, 99
Green Gram Beans, 11, 12
Green Peas, 18, 31, 37, 41, 45, 57, 65, 87, 93, 101

H

Haricot Beans, 11, 28, 29, 57, 105

I

Indian Rice, 7, 8

J

Japanese Rice, 7, 8, 104
Jasmine Rice, 7, 8, 104

K

Kidney Beans, 11, 12, 13, 69, 76, 77

L

Lamb, 5, 17, 29, 53, 57, 63, 83, 89, 104
Lemon, 16, 19, 31, 73, 75, 77, 93
Lentils, 11, 12, 52, 53, 55, 58, 59, 85, 87, 98, 99
Lima Beans, 11, 39, 88, 89
Lime, 19, 99
Loin of Lamb, 17

Loin of Pork, 17
Long Grain Rice, 5, 7, 8, 23, 104

M

Madagascar Beans, 11
Marjoram, 16, 25, 35, 37, 45, 51, 53, 55, 63, 69, 79, 91
Meats, 5, 6, 17, 104
Medium Grain Rice, 8, 104
Mexican Beans, 11
Mexican Black Beans, 12
Mince, 5, 17
Mochi Rice, 8
Mung Beans, 11, 12, 48, 49, 79
Mung Peas, 12
Mungo Beans, 12
Mushrooms, 18, 27, 39, 41, 43, 45, 49, 51, 57, 59, 67, 71, 77, 81, 87, 91, 97, 99, 101
Mustard Powder, 16, 71

N

Nutmeg, 16, 53, 71

O

Olive Oil, 15, 19, 63, 65, 73, 75, 106
Onion, 25, 27, 29, 31, 33, 35, 37, 39, 41, 43, 45, 47, 49, 51, 53, 55, 57, 59, 61, 63, 65, 67, 69, 71, 73, 75, 77, 79, 81, 83, 85, 87, 89, 91, 93, 95, 97, 99, 101, 103
Onions, 5, 6, 14, 15, 18, 105, 106
Orange, 19, 71, 77, 93
Oregano, 16, 29, 33, 37, 39, 41, 43, 63, 65, 73, 75, 79, 85, 89

P

Paella Rice, 8
Paprika, 16, 29, 63, 77, 89, 93
Parsley, 16, 65, 77
Pearl Rice, 8
Pearled Rice, 8
Pidgeon Peas, 12, 81, 103
Piedmount Rice, 8
Pigeon Peas, 12, 81, 102, 103
Pinto Beans, 12, 83, 92, 93
Plain Boiled Rice, 5, 23
Pork, 5, 17, 31, 33, 75, 79, 99, 104
Prawns, 5, 17, 35, 49, 51, 55, 65, 67, 81, 87, 91, 95, 103, 104, 106
Puy Lentils, 12, 52, 53, 85

R

Rajma Beans, 11, 12
Red Onions, 14
Resecoco Beans, 12
Rice, 1, 5, 6, 7, 8, 22, 23, 24, 25, 26, 27, 29, 30, 31, 32, 33, 34, 35, 36, 37, 38, 39, 40, 41, 42, 43, 44, 45, 47, 49, 50, 51, 53, 54, 55, 56, 57, 59, 61, 63, 65, 67, 68, 69, 71, 73, 75, 77, 78, 79, 80, 81, 82, 83, 84, 85, 86, 87, 89, 90, 91, 93, 94, 95, 97, 99, 101, 103, 104

Risotto Rice, 7, 8
Roman Beans, 12
Rosemary, 16, 53, 63
Round Grain Rice, 8
Rump Steak, 17
Runner Cannellini, 10, 13

S

Salt, 16, 25, 27, 31, 33, 35, 37, 39, 41, 43, 45, 47, 49, 51, 55, 57, 59, 61, 63, 65, 67, 69, 71, 73, 75, 77, 81, 85, 87, 91, 95, 97, 99, 103
Salugia Beans, 10, 13
Sausages, 5, 17, 104
Savoury Mince, 5
Sesame Oil, 19, 47, 49, 67, 99
Shell Beans, 13
Short Grain Rice, 8, 104
Soy Beans, 13
Soy Sauce, 19, 47, 49, 67, 99
Soya Beans, 13, 60, 61, 91
Spanish Black Beans, 9, 13
Spanish Rice, 8
Split Peas, 13, 70, 71, 95
Spring Onions, 14
Sticky Rice, 8
Stock Cube, 19
Sushi Rice, 8
Sweet Corn, 18, 25, 29, 31, 33, 37, 47, 55, 61, 65, 69, 75, 79, 81, 83, 85, 89
Sweet Rice, 7, 8

T

Thai Basmati Rice, 7, 8
Thai Jasmine Rice, 7, 8
Thyme, 16, 27, 29, 31, 33, 35, 41, 45, 53, 55, 57, 63, 65, 83, 87
Tomato Puree, 19
Tomatoes, 18, 27, 29, 31, 35, 37, 39, 41, 43, 45, 51, 53, 57, 61, 63, 65, 73, 75, 83, 91, 97, 101, 103, 105, 107
Turtle Beans, 10, 13

V

Vegetable Oil, 19, 106
Vegetarians, 5, 17, 104

W

Waxy Rice, 8
White Kidney Beans, 13
White Onions, 14
White Rice, 7, 8
Whole Grain Rice, 7, 8
Wild Rice, 7, 8, 104
Windsor Beans, 13

Y

Yellow Onions, 14, 18, 105

Beecroft Publishing
Beecroft
Crittenden Road
Matfield, Kent
TN12 7EQ
United Kingdom

www.beecroftpublishing.co.uk

email: sales@beecroftpublishing.co.uk

EU Authorised Representative:
Easy Access System Europe
Mustamäe tee 50, 10621 Tallinn, Estonia

www.ingramcontent.com/pod-product-compliance
Lightning Source LLC
LaVergne TN
LVHW070838080426
835510LV00030B/3442